I Needed to Hear That: Wisdom I Didn't Ask for but God Gave Anyway

A 7-Week Devotional Walk Through Proverbs

by Kimberly Billings

**FAVOR DEI
PRESS**
NEW YORK
GRACE-FUELED. FAITH-FILLED.
FULLY CAFFEINATED.

I Needed to Hear That:
Wisdom I Didn't Ask for but God Gave Anyway

First Edition

Library of Congress Control Number: TBD

Cover Designer: Kimberly Billings

ISBN: 979-8-9993690-1-7

Printed in United States of America

I Needed to Hear That: A 7-Week Walk Through Proverbs

Week 7 – Living Legacy

Epilogue

Prologue: Why Proverbs, Why Now

When I first started digging into Proverbs, it wasn't because I thought the world needed yet another devotional book. Honestly, it was because *I needed* it. I needed wisdom. I needed direction. I needed the kind of callouts only God's Word can deliver. Proverbs has this way of holding up a mirror and saying, "Yep, this one's for you, my friend." I didn't want to just read those words and nod along politely. I wanted to absorb them, wrestle with them. I wanted to laugh, cry, roll my eyes, and ultimately let them do what God intended: shape my heart. Every time I read Proverbs it slaps me upside the head because I know deep down *I needed to hear that.*

As I started jotting down my reflections, I realized something: maybe I'm not the only one who needs this. Maybe you've rolled your eyes at yourself, too. Maybe you've needed a reminder that wisdom is for everyday life: standing at the kitchen sink, sitting at a light in the minivan, observing the office drama, enjoying the friendships and even the family chaos (although that last one can be both good and bad at times, am I right?). Proverbs doesn't sail past all of that; it dives head first into it.

So, this isn't me handing you wisdom like I've figured it all out. Nope. This is me saying, "Hey, come, grab some coffee and sit. Let's dig deep, laugh at ourselves, cry when it gets real, and most importantly, let God's Word call us out and lead us forward."

If there's one thing I do know for sure: when God says, "This is the way of wisdom," He means it, and He means it for *you*, too.

Prayer to Begin

Lord, You know me. You know how I trip over the same stuff again and again, how I get in my own way, and how I try to out-think You (yeah, like THAT ever works). I'm coming to Proverbs because I clearly don't have it all figured out, and I don't want to pretend I do. I want Your wisdom. I *need* Your wisdom. So, call me out when I need it, comfort me when I'm a mess, and keep nudging (pushing? slapping? kicking?) me closer to You. Let this study not just be words on a page, but truth in my bones. Amen.

Bottom line

I didn't pick Proverbs because I have it all together. I picked it because I clearly don't.

WEEK 1 – Wisdom Starts Here

Stop winging it and start walking with God.

Day 1 – Why We're Here

Verse: Proverbs 1:7 - *The fear of the Lord is the beginning of knowledge; fools despise wisdom and instruction.*

Let's Dig In

Here's the thing: most of us like to believe we've got life figured out by now (typically if you're between the ages of 18 and 23 or beyond 50 – change my mind). We've lived through storms, learned a few lessons, maybe even picked up some wisdom we like to dish out to others (whether they asked for it or not). Add in podcasts, books, Google, and the never-ending supply of opinions on social media, and we're swimming (drowning?) in "wisdom." Then Proverbs 1:7 cuts through all of it with one sharp line: if God isn't at the center, it's not wisdom, it's just noise.

This verse is the starting line. Proverbs doesn't give us a warm-up lap, it plants a flag and makes us choose: are we going to live in awe-filled reverence of God, letting Him be our source of wisdom, or are we going to keep circling the same old track of self-reliance? Spoiler alert: one path works. The other one ends in regret.

Now, let's clear up that phrase, "fear of the Lord." It doesn't mean hiding in a corner waiting for God to zap you when you mess up. It's about reverence, respect, and remembering *He's God* and *we're not*. It's trusting His guardrails, even when they don't make sense yet. It's admitting His ways are better, even when ours feel more reasonable in the moment.

Notice what the verse says: *it's the beginning of knowledge*. You don't even get motoring down the road to wisdom until you *start* with Him. Which means this whole seven-week study isn't about collecting cute quotes to post on your Instagram. It's about letting God dig deep, expose our pride, and rewire the "I've got this" mindset that keeps creeping back (because you KNOW it will!).

If I'm honest, I've tried the other way. Maybe you have, too. I've relied heavily on my own smarts, thought I could figure it out, pushed ahead without asking God. Every single time, it left me exhausted or empty. We've all hustled, worried, and overthought ourselves into the ground (no one's a better over-thinker than me). Still, God always steps in with an invitation: "Start fresh! Start with Me!" Let's always make an effort to accept that invitation!

So, here's where we land today, our first day together on our wisdom journey: it doesn't start with us. It starts with God. Until we make that shift, until we stop relying on our own "bright ideas" and surrender to His real ones, we're just stuck in the mud and spinning our wheels.

Let's Reflect

- Where are you still acting like you know better than God?
- Think of a time when your "I've got this" approach flopped. What did you learn?
- How could fearing the Lord-really respecting Him and His will *first*-change the way you handle your words, choices, or relationships?

Let's Pray

Lord, I'll admit it: I like to act like I know what I'm doing. (You know how often *that* backfires.) I don't want to keep running in circles. Teach me to *start* with You, not just drag You in *after* I've made a mess. Pull me back when I wander into self-reliance and give me a heart that's willing to learn. Thank You for never giving up on me and for inviting me into *Your* wisdom, the only thing that truly works. Amen.

Bottom line

If God's not in it, it's just noise. Start with Him. Period.

Day 2 – *God Gets the Final Word*

Verse: Proverbs 9:10 - *The fear of the Lord is the beginning of wisdom, and the knowledge of the Holy One is insight.*

Let's Dig In

Yesterday we talked about the starting line: wisdom begins with God. Today takes it a step further: wisdom grows when we actually get to know Him. Proverbs 9:10 ties the two together. The fear of the Lord is where it starts, but it deepens into *insight* when we walk with Him daily. Daily? Yes, daily. Got it? Ok, good, moving on.

Think about it like this: respect is the doorway, but relationship is the house (good one, huh? I know!). You can recognize that *God* is God and *you* aren't (that's fear of the Lord), but real wisdom is shaped as you learn His heart, His ways, His voice. The more you know Him, the more sense everything else starts to make.

Here's where we hit the tension: there are so many competing voices swirling around in our brains. Culture has a voice. Social media has a voice. Our own desires have a voice. Oh, and get a load of this one: people we care about have voices too, and sometimes they sound more convincing than God's (duh, you knew that). If you're not careful, those voices become the filter you run your decisions through. You end up listening to everyone except the One who actually knows where the path leads.

Wisdom isn't about having all the right answers; it's about knowing the right Voice who DOES. That's humbling, my friend, because we'd often rather keep God in the *background* until we need a quick opinion. Real wisdom means He gets the first and final word every time, even when it's not the word we wanted to hear.

I've learned this the hard way, and I STILL don't go to Him first all the time. Maybe you know what I'm talking about? There have been times I ignored the nudge of godly wisdom (Holy Spirit, is that You?) and realized too late that I should've listened. On the flip side, there have been times I DID choose to follow His lead even when it didn't make sense, and later saw clearly *why* His way was better. That's the difference between insight and hindsight. One saves you from the crash; the other just shows you the wreckage. (Oooh, another good one!)

This verse is also a good reminder that knowing *about* God isn't the same as *knowing* Him. You can memorize verses, go to church every week, or even lead Bible studies (you know, check all the boxes) and still miss the point if you're not actually walking with Him. Insight comes from relationship, not résumé.

So, here's the challenge for today: if wisdom starts with reverence (Day 1), then it grows with relationship (Day 2). Let God be the filter for every voice you hear. Let Him be the first and final word on every decision. Don't just *start* the journey with Him, *stick* with Him.

Let's Reflect

- Which voices have been shaping your decisions more lately: God's or the world's?

- When did you realize too late that you ignored godly wisdom?

- How might your choices look different if you filtered every piece of advice through God's Word?

Let's Pray

Lord, there are so many voices trying to guide me, but I want Yours to be the loudest. Help me know You more so that my choices reflect Your wisdom, not just my faulty instincts. Give me a heart that listens, a mind that discerns, and the humility to follow even when it's hard. Thank You that real insight comes from knowing You, not from figuring it all out myself. Amen.

Bottom line

Wisdom doesn't stop at the starting line, it grows with every step you take closer to God.

Day 3 – *Trust Issues*

Verse: Proverbs 3:5-6 - *Trust in the Lord with all your heart, and do not lean on your own understanding. In all your ways acknowledge him, and he will make straight your paths.*

Let's Dig In

If trusting God came naturally, we wouldn't need this reminder. To be honest, we wouldn't need this book and I'd likely be binging something on Netflix (we all know I wouldn't elect to fold all that laundry). Proverbs 3:5–6 is one of those verses we love to quote but living it out is a whole different story. Trust the Lord with all your heart. Don't lean on your own understanding. Sounds simple enough, until God's plan doesn't look anything like yours.

Here's the truth: leaning on our own understanding feels easier. It's what we know. We can control it, map it out, weigh the pros and cons, run the numbers, and convince ourselves we're on the right track. Control feels safe. Waiting on God does not. Yet this proverb is clear: your way may feel logical, but His way is the one that will ultimately work. (For the record, I'm not saying that you and God will never be on the same page and that you're always going to be wrong, but for this devotion, roll with it, ok?)

Think of the steering wheel in your car. When you're driving, your hands are locked on tight. You know where you want to go, how fast you want to get there, and the route you think makes sense. Trusting God means loosening that grip and letting Him take control of the wheel. (Good theme for a song!) Sometimes that means a detour. Sometimes that means a stop you didn't plan on. Sometimes that means the route takes longer than you'd like. Still, the promise is that, if you acknowledge Him, He will make your path straight. Not necessarily easy, but purposeful.

Most of us (all of us?) can look back and see times when our plans fell apart. We thought we had the perfect solution, only to end up in a dead end. We've also had those moments where we followed God's lead even when it made zero sense to us, and later realized He was protecting us, guiding us, or preparing us for something we couldn't see. That's the difference between trusting our own understanding and trusting Him. One leaves us frustrated; the other brings peace even when we don't know why.

It's worth noting that this verse says "all your heart". Not just the safe parts. Not the Sunday morning parts. All of it. Trusting God means handing over the pieces you've been clutching, the relationship you're scared to let go of, the future you're trying to script yourself, the fears you replay at night at 2am. Those aren't off-limits to Him. He wants them, too.

So, here's today's challenge: unclench your fists. Stop trying to white-knuckle your way through life. Tell God you're done "backseat driving" (then actually follow through). He knows the map better than you do, and He's never lost.

Let's Reflect

- What's one area of your life you've been gripping too tightly, trying to control?
- How do you usually react when God's plan doesn't make sense to you?

16

- What could change if you trusted Him with all your heart, not just the safe parts?

Let's Pray

Lord, You *know* how much I like control. I hold on so tightly to my plans, even though I know they're limited and very often flawed. Help me to release what I've been gripping too hard. Teach me to trust You with the parts of my heart I've tried to keep for myself. Thank You that, even when the path feels unclear, You already see the whole route. Amen.

Bottom line

Stop backseat-driving God.

Day 4 – *Don't Be a Know-It-All*

Verse: Proverbs 3:7 – *Be not wise in your own eyes; fear the Lord and turn away from evil.*

Let's Dig In

Let's be real: the easiest person to fool is yourself. We're experts at it. We can spin a situation, rationalize our decisions, and convince ourselves we're fine even when we're heading straight into trouble. Proverbs 3:7 doesn't sugarcoat it: "Be not wise in your own eyes." In other words, stop believing your own press.

Being wise in your own eyes can show up in different ways. Maybe it's brushing off advice because you're *sure* you know better. Maybe it's excusing a compromise with "it's not a big deal." Maybe it's ignoring God's urging because *your* plan feels more practical. Whatever the version, the root is the same: pride. Pride whispers, "I've got this," even when every red flag says otherwise. Don't worry, I'm preaching to myself here, too.

The verse doesn't leave us stuck with the warning, it gives us the way forward: *fear the Lord and turn away from evil*. Wisdom doesn't mean you never make mistakes. It means you stay humble enough to admit you need God and willing enough to turn when He shows you a better way. That humility is what keeps your heart soft and your steps steady (following His lead).

Here's what I've noticed in my own life: the older I get, the easier it is to think I should have "arrived" by now. I've got years of experience and plenty of lessons behind me, so sometimes I assume I've got the wisdom thing handled. That's dangerous thinking. The moment I believe I don't need reminders or correction anymore, I put myself at risk. God never calls us to outgrow humility. He calls us to remain teachable, no matter how many candles are on the cake.

Think back for a minute. How many regrets in your life were tied to pride? Maybe you ignored wise advice and regretted it later. Maybe you pushed past God's warning signs and ended up in a mess. Maybe you clung to the idea that you could handle it, only to discover you couldn't. Pride blinds us in the moment, but the wreckage is clear afterward (think back to that crash/wreckage thing in Day 2).

The beauty of this verse is that it offers freedom. Humility doesn't box us in; *it keeps us safe*. It keeps our hearts open to correction before we drift too far. It allows God to redirect us without having to let us crash first. *Godly correction is not punishment, it's protection.* It's His way of saying, "I love you too much to let you keep going this direction."

Wisdom isn't about proving how much you know. It's about surrendering what you *think* you know. Real wisdom keeps its knees bent and its heart soft, ready for the detours and plan-changes. It doesn't strut; it listens. It doesn't show off; it leans in. The know-it-all ends up stuck. The teachable one keeps growing.

God's Word: 1   My pride: 0

Let's Reflect

- Where have you been "wise in your own eyes" lately?
- How does humility protect you from slipping into sin?
- What's one practical way you can pause and seek God's wisdom before acting today?

Let's Pray

Lord, I know how easily pride sneaks into my heart. I don't want to live convinced that I know it all while ignoring what You're trying to teach me. Strip away my pride and keep me teachable. Give me the humility to listen, the courage to change, and the wisdom to turn from what pulls me away from You. Thank You for loving me enough to guide me back when I wander. Amen.

Bottom line

Being a know-it-all usually means you don't.

Day 5 – *Heart Guard*

Verse: Proverbs 4:23 – *Keep your heart with all vigilance, for from it flow the springs of life.*

Let's Dig In

Your heart is the control center of your life. It's more than feelings or emotions. It's the core of who you are, the place that shapes your choices, your words, your priorities. That's why Proverbs says, "above all else" guard it. Everything flows from there. Strap yourself in, this one is gonna be a doozy.

Here's the reality: *what you let in will eventually come out*. Fear, bitterness, or lies can sneak in like weeds and take root before you even realize it. Given enough time, they choke out joy, peace, and truth. Jesus said it too: "Out of the abundance of the heart the mouth speaks" (Luke 6:45). The sharp words that slip out, the resentment that lingers, the negativity that colors your outlook; those started as seeds in your heart long before anyone else noticed. Think about how much simpler relationships often were before social media came onto the scene. Scrolling isn't self-care, it's often self-sabotage. Ask me how I know… actually, don't.

Guarding your heart doesn't mean building walls or becoming untouchable. It isn't about isolating yourself or shutting people out (or deleting your social media accounts). It's about setting holy boundaries. Picture it like a garden. If you care about what grows there, you protect it. You pull weeds before they take over. You fence it in so it doesn't get trampled. You don't just let anything plant itself in your soil.

Think about what it looks like to let garbage in. Maybe it's the shows you binge that glorify what you know isn't good for your soul. Maybe it's the conversations you replay over and over until bitterness takes root. Maybe it's scrolling for hours and realizing you're left jealous, drained, or angry. None of these things seem huge in the moment, but they pile up until your heart is cluttered with junk.

On the flip side, guarding your heart means being intentional about what you *allow* to shape you. It might look like turning off a show that stirs up things you don't need in your mind. It might mean stepping back from a friendship that drags you into gossip. It might mean limiting how much news you consume because it fuels fear more than faith. Boundaries like these aren't about being uptight. They're about wisdom. They're about protecting what God says is the "wellspring of your life".

There's another layer here, too. Guarding your heart isn't just for *your* sake. What flows out of your heart spills into the lives of the people around you as well. If your heart is full of joy, peace, and truth, that's what overflows into your relationships. If it's full of anger, bitterness, and lies, that spills out too. Guarding your heart is one of the most loving things you can do for others, because everything you let in eventually flows back out. Makes perfect sense, doesn't it?

So, here's today's reminder: pay attention to what you're feeding your heart. If you wouldn't want it shaping your words or your actions, it doesn't belong inside. Protect the soil so good things can grow!

Let's Reflect

- What's one negative influence you've let into your heart?
- How does protecting your heart help you protect others?
- Which boundaries might you need to tighten this week?

Let's Pray

God, I know how quickly my heart can get cluttered with things that don't honor You. I let in distractions, negativity, and lies without realizing how much they shape me. Help me guard my heart with wisdom. Show me where I need better boundaries, and give me the courage to set them. Thank You for caring about my heart and for shaping it to reflect Your goodness and truth. Amen.

Bottom Line

Garbage in, garbage out; so, stop letting it in.

Day 6 – *Ask the Ant*

Verse: Proverbs 6:6 - *Go to the ant, O sluggard; consider her ways and be wise.*

Let's Dig In

Ants are not glamorous. Nobody writes poems about ants. Nobody brags about watching ants work (ok, not 100% true… I actually have a friend who totally admires ants and even has a tattoo of one… don't judge, he's cool). Yet Proverbs points us right to them as role models for wisdom. Why? Ants have something most of us struggle with: *diligence*.

Think about it. Ants don't need a boss standing over them with a checklist. They don't need pep talks, rewards, or deadlines. They simply get up and do what needs to be done. They prepare in the summer, so they'll have food in the winter. No excuses. No stalling. They just do the work.

This verse isn't knocking down-time and rest. God designed rest as a gift, and Scripture tells us to honor it. (Another friend of mine likes to text me when it's "nap time"… because I'm not retired yet and apparently that's amusing). The warning here is against laziness, procrastination, and that "I'll get to it later" mindset that so easily creeps in. Laziness doesn't look dramatic at first. It looks like hitting snooze one more time, scrolling instead of praying, or pushing off that project God's been pushing you to finish. Before long, those little habits pile up into a lifestyle of delay.

We all have areas where we've been dragging our feet. Maybe God's asked you to mend a relationship, but you've been waiting for the "right moment." Maybe He's been nudging you to step out in faith, but you keep telling yourself you're not ready. Maybe it's as simple as a daily discipline: prayer, Scripture, healthy eating choices that you keep promising yourself you'll "start tomorrow". Meanwhile, the ants are out there making progress and that pile of clean laundry on your bed isn't folding itself.

Diligence doesn't always mean big, dramatic moves. More often, it looks like small, faithful steps. Writing a page. Making a phone call. Setting aside ten minutes to pray instead of scrolling. Those small choices rarely feel impressive in the moment, yet they build momentum. Over time, they shape character, strengthen faith, and prepare you for the future God already sees coming.

There's another lesson tucked in here too. Ants don't work alone. They carry loads together, each doing their part. What would crush one ant becomes manageable because of the community around it. God designed us the same way! Diligence isn't just personal grit, it's also leaning into the people He's placed in our lives. Faithful work isn't meant to be a solo performance; it's a team effort.

So, today, maybe the challenge isn't to do everything at once. Maybe it's simply to *start*. Take the small step God's been putting on your heart. Move forward even if it feels tiny. Faithful diligence doesn't always get applause, but it honors God, and it prepares you for tomorrow in ways you can't yet see. *Boom* mic drop

God isn't calling you to burnout. He's calling you to faithfulness. He isn't asking you to sprint; He's asking you to keep moving, step by steady step. Even the ants get that much right.

Let's Reflect

- Where have you been procrastinating on something God's called you to do?
- What's one small step you can take toward diligence today?
- How could steady, faithful work bring glory to God in your current season?

Let's Pray

Lord, You know how quick I am to make excuses. I tell myself I'll get to it tomorrow, even when You've made it clear what You want me to do today. Forgive my procrastination. Teach me the steady diligence of the ant. Show me the small steps that I can take right now, and give me the courage to actually take them. Thank You that faithful work, even when no one notices, can bring You glory. Amen.

Bottom Line

If an ant can do it, so can you.

Day 7 – *The Pride Problem*

Verse: Proverbs 11:2 – *When pride comes, then comes disgrace, but with the humble is wisdom.*

Let's Dig In

As though we haven't had enough of the pride stuff so far, we're gonna get back into it again. Pride is sneaky. It's easy to spot in someone else, but hard to see in ourselves. We tend to picture it as the loud, braggy kind, someone who always has to prove they're the best or win every conversation. Pride looks like that sometimes, but sometimes it even slips in quietly. It shows up when we forget we need God, when we trust our plan more than His, or when we decide we're strong enough to handle life on our own.

Proverbs 11:2 tells it straight: *pride leads to disgrace.* Maybe not right away, but eventually pride catches up with us. It blinds us to reality, makes us unteachable, and sets us up for a fall. Pride whispers, "You've got this," while the ground beneath your feet is already cracking.

Humility, on the other hand, opens the door for wisdom. Humility isn't thinking less of yourself, it's thinking of yourself *accurately.* It remembers that God is *God* and you are *not.* It doesn't shrink back from truth, but it does leave space for grace, learning, and correction. Where pride slams the door in God's face, humility swings it wide open and says, "Come in. Teach me. Lead me."

The tricky thing is that humility often grows in places that don't feel good. It grows when you admit you were wrong. It grows when you listen instead of defending yourself. It grows when you choose to serve instead of being served. None of those things are comfortable, but they're the very soil where God plants wisdom.

Think about it: how many regrets in your life tie back to pride? Times you ignored advice because you thought you knew better. Times you refused to apologize and let a relationship dissolve. Times you insisted on your own way and ended up stuck in a mess you could have avoided. Pride blinds us in the moment but leaves us very much aware after the fact. (#wreckage)

Now flip it around. Think of the people you admire most. Chances are they're not the flashy, prideful ones. They're the ones who quietly serve, who admit their weaknesses without shame, who listen with a heart ready to learn. That's the power of humility; it reflects the heart of Jesus.

Jesus Himself is the *ultimate* picture of humility. The Son of God left heaven's throne and humbled Himself all the way to the cross! If the King of kings chose humility, what excuse do we have for clinging to pride? Every time we let go of the need to prove ourselves, we look a little more like Him. Every time we open the door to humility, wisdom walks in too.

So, here's today's challenge: pay attention to where pride is trying to sneak into your life. Maybe it's in a conversation where you feel the need to have the last word. Maybe it's in your refusal to ask for help. Maybe it's in that small voice that says, "You don't need to pray about this one, you've got it." Pride will always promise strength, but it always ends in a crash. Humility may feel like the difficult path, but it's the only one that leads to wisdom, peace, and grace.

Let's Reflect

- How has pride tripped you up in the past?
- What's one area where you could intentionally practice humility this week?
- Who in your life models humility well, and what can you learn from them?

Let's Pray

Lord, pride is so easy to spot in others and so hard to see in myself. I don't want to live blinded by it. Help me to love humility the way You do. Teach me to welcome correction, to admit my weaknesses, and to depend fully on You. Protect me from the trap of pride, and grow in me a spirit that reflects Your heart. Amen.

Bottom Line

Pride is a bad investment, it always crashes.

WEEK 2 – Taming the Tongue

Your tongue can be your biggest problem or your biggest witness.

Day 8 – *Words That Heal*

Verse: Proverbs 10:12 – *Hatred stirs up strife, but love covers all offenses.*

Let's Dig In

If it walks like drama and talks like drama… it's drama. Drama doesn't need much help to get going. Hatred loves it. Satan loves it. A harsh word here, a grudge there, and suddenly small sparks turn into full-blown fires. We've all seen it happen (maybe even caught in the middle): one comment in the group chat, one family disagreement, one old wound reopened, and everything is in flames again. Ever send a snarky text to the wrong person, namely the target of that text? (Tell me I'm not the only one!) Well, you guessed it: it instantly turns into drama and Satan is wringing his hands in delight.

Love, on the other hand, does the opposite. Love covers. Love heals. Love speaks life (nod to Toby Mac). That doesn't mean ignoring sin or pretending everything's fine when it's not. It means refusing to weaponize someone else's mistakes. It means choosing forgiveness instead of digging up the past. Love doesn't dump gasoline on the fire; it brings the bucket of water.

This verse is a reminder that *the way we respond matters*. Anyone can stir things up. It takes wisdom and humility to cover instead of expose. Covering an offense doesn't mean you excuse it. It means you refuse to make it bigger. You decide not to fan the flames. You choose peace over payback. This just might be one of the most difficult tasks we're charged with in life. Ouch, right?

I'll be honest, this isn't easy. Our default is usually to defend ourselves, point out how we were wronged, or make sure everyone knows our side of the story. Love calls us higher. Love reminds us that our words can either keep the fight alive or end it for good. Covering in love doesn't make you weak, it makes you wise.

Think of how many relationships could have been saved if love had been chosen over drama or hatred. Think of how many conflicts could have fizzled out if someone had decided not to keep "poking the bear". Love doesn't deny that hurt happened. It simply chooses to heal instead of harm.

Jesus modeled this perfectly. He absorbed the sting of our sin and chose to cover us with His grace instead of allowing to endure the punishment we deserved. If we've received that kind of covering, how could we not offer it to others?

So today, ask yourself: are you stirring or covering? Are your words throwing fuel on the fire or bringing peace to it? Wisdom is knowing which one honors God.

Let's Reflect

- Who in your life needs you to cover an offense instead of stirring it up again?
- What's the difference between covering sin in love and enabling sin in silence?

- How does this verse challenge your default reaction to conflict?

Let's Pray

Lord, You know how quickly I want to defend myself and make sure my side is heard. You know how quick I am sometimes to stir the pot instead of attempting to make peace. Help me choose love instead of drama and hatred. Teach me when to speak truth and when to cover an offense with grace. Thank You for covering *me* with Your love when I deserved judgment. Amen.

Bottom Line

Some fires aren't worth your marshmallows.

Day 9 – *Zip It*

Verse: Proverbs 10:19 – *When words are many, transgression is not lacking, but whoever restrains his lips is prudent.*

Let's Dig In

Bookmark this verse in your Bible before you conveniently "forget" it. Today is gonna sting a bit. Confession: I wanted to skip this verse, but here we are. Color me convicted.

We live in a world that never stops talking. Words are everywhere: comments, posts, texts, emails, hot takes, and rants. The more words, the more likely it is that something foolish slips out. Proverbs 10:19 calls it like it is: when words pile up, sin isn't far behind.

This isn't about staying silent forever. God gave us voices for a reason. Words can encourage, teach, heal, and bless. The problem comes when we forget that words have weight. The more we throw around, the greater the chance we'll regret some of them. Wisdom looks like knowing when to close your mouth. (Some of my friends and family are laughing at me saying this right now.)

Think about how many times you've said something too quickly and wished you could reel it back in. Maybe it was anger, maybe it was gossip, maybe it was just filling silence with nonsense. The damage was done the second the words hit the air, it's like squeezing out toothpaste, you can't shove it back in the tube once it's out.

Restraint is underrated. The world celebrates people who speak fast and speak often. Scripture flips it upside down and says the wise are the ones who know how to hold back. Silence at the right time is not weakness, it's wisdom.

Sometimes restraint means biting your tongue in an argument instead of making the jab that will win the moment but wound the relationship. Sometimes it means listening longer before offering your opinion. Sometimes it's choosing not to post the snarky comment online even though it would feel so satisfying.

Jesus modeled this too. There were moments He stayed silent when He could have defended Himself. That silence was strength. It kept Him aligned with the Father's will and sometimes spared Him from being dragged into distractions and situations that didn't matter. If He could practice holy restraint, so can we.

Here's the good news: every word you don't say can never be used against you. Every harsh thought you keep between you and God is one less wound you have to apologize for. Restraint keeps peace intact. It preserves relationships. It saves you from the regret of saying something you can't unsay.

So, maybe today's wisdom is simple: talk less, listen more. Pray before you post. Pause before you reply. The words you don't speak might be the wisest ones of all.

Let's Reflect

- When have you regretted speaking too soon?
- How can you build the habit of thinking before you speak?

- When has silence been more powerful than words in your life?

Let's Pray

Lord, put a holy filter over my mouth today. Teach me to recognize when my words are needed and when silence would be wiser. Give me the self-control to pause before I speak, so that my words bring life instead of regret. Amen.

Bottom Line

Not every thought needs a microphone.

Day 10 – *Building or Breaking*

Verse: Proverbs 12:4 – *An excellent wife is the crown of her husband, but she who brings shame is like rottenness in his bones.*

Let's Dig In

I'm going to continue on this "harsh and hasty vs. kind and thoughtful words" trend and this verse paints a pretty vivid picture. On one side, you've got a crown: shining, valuable, a sign of honor. On the other side, you've got rot deep down to the bone: slow, painful, and destructive from the inside out. That's the contrast Proverbs uses to describe the influence we can have in our closest relationships.

You don't have to be married to get the point here. The truth applies to every role we play: friend, daughter/son, co-worker, neighbor, church member. Our words and actions either build people up or break them down. We can be a crown that adds value, strength, and encouragement, or we can be a slow decay that drains the people around us.

This is where the tongue comes in. Words are powerful. They can breathe life into someone's weary heart, or they can eat away at their confidence and peace. A single compliment can carry someone for weeks. A single harsh word can replay in their mind for years. We don't always realize how much weight our words carry until we've either lifted someone up or crushed them.

The hard part is that tearing down sometimes feels easier in the moment. Sarcasm comes naturally. Criticism slips out fast. Negativity spreads quickly. (I'm typing this with a side-eye at myself.) Encouragement takes more intentionality. It requires slowing down, noticing the good, and choosing to speak life even when it's not the easy option. Yet Proverbs reminds us that it's worth the effort because the difference between a crown and rottenness isn't small. It's life-shaping.

So, ask yourself: when people walk away from you, do they feel strengthened or weakened? Do they feel honored, or do they feel diminished? None of us get this right all the time, but our patterns matter. If your words consistently drain instead of build, it's time for a heart check. *Out of the overflow of the heart, the mouth speaks.* (Can't take credit for that line, but I don't know who said it either.)

The beauty here is that God gives us the chance to reset. Even if you've spent years being more critical than encouraging, today can be different. You can decide right now to be a crown in someone's life by speaking words that honor, affirm, and uplift. It might feel small, but to the person on the receiving end, it could mean everything.

Let's Reflect

- In your relationships, are you more like a crown or like corrosion?
- What's one way you can bring honor or encouragement to someone close to you this week?

- How have your words shaped the atmosphere in your home, workplace, or friendships?

Let's Pray

God, I want my words to build, not break. Show me where I've been careless or critical and give me the wisdom to use my influence for good. Help me to be a crown in the lives of the people around me, a source of strength, encouragement, and honor. Thank You for speaking life into me through Your Word so that I can pass that life on to others. Amen.

Bottom Line

Crowns shine. Rot spreads.

Day 11 – *Mouth Guard*

Verse: Proverbs 13:3 – *Whoever guards his mouth preserves his life; he who opens wide his lips comes to ruin.*

Let's Dig In

Why stop at two verses about how our mouths get us in a pickle? *(But wait! There's more!)* I know this seems repetitive, and maybe you're sick of hearing it by now, but in all honesty, I needed these mouth-warning verses. So much so that I dedicated an entire week to it!

Look, we wear seatbelts to protect our bodies, passwords to protect our accounts, and locks to protect our homes. Proverbs says we need the same kind of guard for our mouths. Why? Unguarded words are dangerous. They can wreck reputations, ruin relationships, and cause more damage than we ever meant.

"Guarding your mouth" isn't about *never* speaking. It's about paying attention to what comes out. Loose words have a way of escaping quickly, whether it's gossip, anger, sarcasm, or just saying too much. Once they're out, you can't reel them back in. An unguarded mouth is like an unlocked front door. It might seem harmless at first, but eventually trouble walks right in.

This verse draws a sharp line: life or ruin. The one who guards their mouth preserves life. The one who doesn't ends up in a mess. That's not an exaggeration. Think about how many friendships have been wrecked by careless words. Think about how many careers have

40

been derailed by one thoughtless comment. Think about the regrets you carry from things you've said too quickly. Maybe these examples don't apply to you, but I bet you know *someone* who experienced them.

The challenge is that we don't always realize how sharp our words are until after the damage is done. A joke that cut deeper than we meant. A secret we should've kept. A heated outburst we can't take back. Guarding your mouth means slowing down enough to ask, "Is this true? Is it helpful? Is it kind? Or is it just going to make things worse?"

There's also a flip side here. Guarding your mouth preserves life, which means your words can protect and strengthen if you use them wisely. A well-timed encouragement, a gentle correction, or a simple "I'm praying for you" can do more good than you realize. Guarding your mouth doesn't just stop the bad; it makes room for the good.

This is one of those places where self-control shines. It's not flashy, but it's powerful. It shows maturity, wisdom, and discipline. People may never know the words you didn't say, but you'll know the peace that comes from restraint.

So maybe today's wisdom is simple: treat your mouth like something worth protecting. Lock it when you need to. Open it with care. Use it to bring life, not ruin.

Let's Reflect

- How have unguarded words caused damage in your life or in someone else's?
- What practical "locks" could you put in place to help guard your mouth this week?
- How might this verse reshape the way you use social media, texting, or everyday conversations?

Let's Pray

Lord, I don't always realize how much power my words have until after they're spoken. Help me guard my mouth with wisdom and self-control. Keep me from speaking out of anger, pride, or carelessness. Instead, let my words bring life, encouragement, and truth. Lord, keep my words life-giving and my lips on a short leash. Thank You for giving me the ability to speak; teach me to use it wisely. Amen.

Bottom Line

Don't leave your mouth unlocked.

Day 12 – *Your Circle Shapes You*

Verse: Proverbs 13:20 – *Whoever walks with the wise becomes wise, but the companion of fools will suffer harm.*

Let's Dig In

Your friends are your future. That's not just a catchy line, it's straight out of Proverbs. The people you spend the most time with are shaping you, whether you know it or not. Their habits, their outlook, their priorities, even their speech, it all rubs off on you. Walk with the wise, and wisdom becomes contagious. Stick with fools, and their recklessness will eventually drag you down. Do you have a few groups of friends with very different personalities or ways of life? Examine your own behavior when you're with each one. Are *you* different?

We love to think we're strong enough to resist bad influences. "I won't be like them, I'll just hang out and stay myself." That's not how it works. The truth is, the people closest to you have influence over you, whether you like it or not. Scripture isn't shy about this; companionship is shaping your character, for better or worse.

So, take a look at your circle. Who are you letting speak into your life? Who are you giving access to your heart and your time? Are they pushing you closer to God or pulling you further away? If your closest voices are full of negativity, foolishness, or sin, it's only a matter of time before that spills into your own life.

Here's the good news: the opposite is also true. Walking with the wise also makes *you* wise. Surrounding yourself with people who love God, speak truth, and live with integrity will lift you higher. Their wisdom becomes your wisdom. Their encouragement fuels your faith. Their example shows you what it looks like to walk closely with God in real life.

This doesn't mean you cut out everyone who isn't "perfect." Jesus spent time with all kinds of people, especially the "imperfect". The difference is, *He* influenced *them* more than *they* influenced *Him*. You can love and serve people who don't share your faith, but your inner circle, the people you lean on most, needs to be made up of those who will strengthen, not weaken, your walk with God.

Think about your closest friendships. Do they make you more patient, more kind, more faithful? Or do they leave you drained, bitter, or careless? Your circle is shaping your future, one conversation and one choice at a time.

So, here's today's challenge: do a little circle check. Notice who you're walking with and where they're leading you. If you want more wisdom, get around wise people. If you want to grow closer to God, spend time with people who are chasing Him. Choose your company wisely; your life depends on it more than you realize. Don't forget, though, your own presence in someone's life just may be the life-giving wisdom *they* need.

Let's Reflect

- Who in your life consistently points you toward wisdom and closer to God?

- Who might be pulling you in the wrong direction right now?
- What's one intentional step you could take to strengthen your inner circle?

Let's Pray

God, thank You for the gift of friendships and community. Show me clearly who I should be walking with closely in this season. Give me the courage to create distance from influences that pull me away from You, and surround me with people who make me wiser, not weaker. Help me also be the kind of friend who lifts others up and points them to You. Amen.

Bottom Line

If you're the smartest person in your crew, get a new crew.

Day 13 – *Slow Burn*

Verse: Proverbs 14:29 – *Whoever is slow to anger has great understanding, but he who has a hasty temper exalts folly.*

Let's Dig In

Quick tempers feel justified in the moment. Something pushes your buttons, and before you even think, the words are out, the tone is sharp, and the damage is done. Proverbs says that kind of hasty anger doesn't show strength, it puts foolishness on display for everyone to see.

Being slow to anger doesn't mean you never feel it. Anger itself isn't *always* wrong. There are things in this world worth being upset about: sin, injustice, cruelty. The issue is when anger becomes our first reaction instead of a carefully measured response. A quick temper rarely produces anything good. It usually leaves a trail of regret, broken trust, or wounded people. Ever regret the words you didn't eat instead? *gulp*

Slowing your anger is wisdom in action. It means you've learned to pause long enough to think, pray, and measure your words before they fly. That pause is where understanding lives. It's the difference between escalating a conflict and diffusing it. A hot head makes bad decisions. A cool head makes wise ones. Someone put that on a coffee mug.

We all know the fallout of letting anger run unchecked. Words we wish we could take back. Silent treatments that drag on for days. Broken relationships that could have been saved if only someone had paused before exploding. Proverbs calls us to something better.

Jesus modeled patience, even when people mocked, accused, or misunderstood Him. If anyone ever had the right to blow up, it was Him. Yet He chose self-control. That's strength. That's wisdom.

Think of it this way: every moment of anger is like holding a match. You can either drop it on gasoline and set everything on fire, or you can blow it out before it spreads. The choice is yours.

So, today's challenge is simple, but not easy: slow down. Take the pause. Count to ten, pray a quick prayer, walk away if you have to. That pause could save a relationship, protect your witness, and keep you from a mountain of regret.

Let's Reflect

- What situations trigger your temper most often?
- How could slowing your reaction change the outcome the next time you feel anger rising?
- When has patience spared you from regret?

Let's Pray

Lord, You know how quickly my temper can flare. Teach me to be slow to anger and quick to listen. Give me the self-control to pause before I react, and fill me with understanding instead of foolishness.

Thank You for showing patience with me every single day. Help me extend that same patience to others. Amen.

Bottom Line

Don't set yourself on fire just to make a point.

Day 14 – *Tone Matters*

Verse: Proverbs 15:1 – *A soft answer turns away wrath, but a harsh word stirs up anger.*

Let's Dig In

Words matter, but so does the way they're delivered. You can say the exact same sentence in two different tones and get two completely different results. Proverbs 15:1 tells us plainly: a soft answer can calm a storm, while a harsh one can spark a wildfire.

Tone is often the difference between someone shutting down and someone opening up. Harsh words put people on defense immediately. They make the walls go up, and once the walls are up, nothing gets through. A gentle tone, on the other hand, lowers the guard. It creates space for listening, for honesty, and for healing.

This doesn't mean avoiding hard truths! Scripture never tells us to water down what's right. After all, we're instructed to call each other out on our wrong doings (um, yup… it's in Scripture: *Brothers, if anyone is caught in any transgression, you who are spiritual should restore him in a spirit of gentleness. Keep watch on yourself, lest you too be tempted. Bear one another's burdens and so fulfill the law of Christ. Galatians 6:1-2).* It means delivering truth in a way that people can actually receive. The goal isn't just to be right, it's to bring peace, wisdom, and restoration. You can be 100% correct and still be wrong in the way you say it.

We've all been on both sides of this. Maybe you've had someone speak a hard truth to you, but their gentleness made you willing to listen instead of fight back. Or maybe you've been in an argument where you had a valid point, but your harsh tone stirred up more anger than clarity. The words were right, but the delivery canceled them out. Consider that a fail.

Think about Jesus. He spoke truth without compromise, yet people who felt crushed by life wanted to be near Him. Why? His tone wasn't condemning! It was firm, yes, but also full of compassion and grace. That's the kind of balance we're called to.

So, here's today's challenge: pay attention to your tone. Not just your words, but how you're saying them. Are your words stirring up peace or stirring up anger? Wisdom knows the difference and chooses carefully (and never does this stuff over text message).

Let's Reflect

- How has your tone escalated a situation in the past? Has someone spoken to you in a tone that made you react poorly?
- When have you seen a gentle response calm tension instead of stirring it up?
- What's one way you can practice speaking truth in love today?

Let's Pray

God, I know my tone can make or break my words. Help me speak in a way that brings peace, not conflict. Teach me to deliver truth with gentleness so that others can actually *hear* it. Thank You for the way Jesus combined grace and truth perfectly. Make me more like Him in the way I speak. Amen.

Bottom Line

You can be right and still be wrong if your tone is trash.

WEEK 3 – Walking the Path

God's GPS never reroutes you wrong.

Day 15 – *Commit It*

Verse: Proverbs 16:3 – *Commit your work to the Lord, and your plans will be established.*

Let's Dig In

We're planners by nature. We make lists, set goals, color-code calendars, and strategize how to get everything done. None of that is bad, it can even be wise, but Proverbs 16:3 reminds us that planning only goes so far. If we don't place our work in God's hands first, we're just spinning our wheels.

To "commit" your work to the Lord isn't the same as giving Him a quick nod before you dive in. It's laying it down completely. It's saying, "God, this is Yours. Shape it, slow it, or scrap it if You need to." That's a lot different from, "Here's my plan, God, please bless it."

The truth is, we don't always know what's best. Our plans can look brilliant on paper and still lead us into frustration. God sees the bigger picture. He knows what's around the corner and where each step will lead. Committing our work to Him means trusting His wisdom over our own, even when it changes the timeline or outcome we had in mind. You wanted wisdom, right? Congratulations, it showed up as inconvenience.

This isn't easy. We like control. We like the satisfaction of checking off our boxes and seeing progress. Letting God redirect us feels uncomfortable, especially when it slows us down or takes us in a direction we wouldn't have chosen. Yet Proverbs promises that if we commit our work to Him, our plans will be established. That doesn't mean every dream we have will come true. It means our work will have purpose, direction, and blessing because it's aligned with His will.

Think about it: how many times have you worked yourself into exhaustion on something, only to realize it wasn't what God wanted for you in the first place? Compare that to the peace of knowing you're right where He's called you to be, even if it doesn't look impressive to anyone else. Established doesn't mean flashy. It means steady, rooted, and fruitful.

So, here's the challenge (not just for today either!): stop asking God to bless a mess you made without Him. Start by handing Him your plans before you put them in motion. Let Him set the direction, and trust that His establishment is better than your hustle.

Let's Reflect

- What's one area of your life you've been running solo instead of committing to God?
- How would full surrender change the way you approach your work?
- What does "established" success look like in God's eyes compared to yours?

Let's Pray

Lord, I don't want to keep working myself into exhaustion on plans that don't line up with Yours. Teach me to commit my work to *You* first, not after the fact. Give me the humility to let You shape, redirect, or even shut down my plans if that's what's best. Thank You for establishing what I place in Your hands. Amen.

Bottom Line

Don't ask God to bless a mess you made without Him.

Day 16 – *Step by Step*

Verse: Proverbs 16:9 – *The heart of man plans his way, but the Lord establishes his steps.*

Let's Dig In

My husband always says, "Man plans, God laughs." We're not wrong to make plans. In fact, planning can be wise. The problem is when we act like our plan is king. Proverbs 16:9 reminds us that God is the One who *truly* directs the journey. We can chart out the route all we want, but He's the One who knows which steps will actually get us where we need to be. (Note, I said where we *need* to be and not where we *want* to be!)

This verse is both comforting and frustrating. Comforting, because it means we're not left to figure out life alone. Frustrating, because God's steps don't always match our neatly drawn map. Sometimes His path is straight and clear. Other times it zig-zags, detours, or takes the scenic route through places we never would've chosen.

Think back on your life. How many times did your "perfect plan" get derailed, only for you to realize later that God was protecting or redirecting you? Maybe it was a job that fell through, a relationship that didn't work out, a series of red lights when you're late to work, or simply a door that closed when you desperately wanted it open. At the time, it felt like disappointment. Later, you could see God's fingerprints all over it. His steps don't always make sense in the moment, but they are always purposeful.

The challenge is trust. We love to map out the destination, but God is more interested in shaping us along the way. Each step is about more than just getting somewhere, it's about becoming someone, the person He wants us to be. He uses the detours, delays, and unexpected turns to grow patience, strengthen faith, and teach dependence on Him.

This doesn't mean we stop planning. It means we hold our plans loosely. We plan with open hands, ready for God to edit, reroute, or rewrite as He sees fit. Our job is to take the next faithful step, not to demand control of the whole journey.

So, here's today's reminder: don't despise the detours. Don't assume a delay means disaster. God is establishing your steps, even when the path doesn't match your picture. Step by step, He's leading you where you need to go. Don't toss your color-coded planner in the garbage, just use pencil instead.

Let's Reflect

- Where have you seen God reroute your plans for the better?
- How does this verse change the way you think about detours and delays?
- What's one area where you need to let God lead instead of clinging to your own plan?

Let's Pray

God, I like to plan, and I like to feel in control. Teach me to trust You with the steps I can't see yet. Help me hold my plans loosely and follow wherever You lead. Thank You that even when the path doesn't match my expectations, You are establishing each step with purpose. Amen.

Bottom Line

Your plan B might be God's plan A.

Day 17 – *Strength Under Control*

Verse: Proverbs 16:32 – *Whoever is slow to anger is better than the mighty, and he who rules his spirit than he who takes a city.*

Let's Dig In

The world loves to celebrate big, flashy strength and presence. The loudest voice, the boldest move, the biggest win, that's what usually gets the spotlight, right? Proverbs flips that idea on its head. Real strength isn't about conquering cities or crushing opponents. It's about self-control. According to God's wisdom, the one who can keep their cool is stronger than the one who wins a battle. Yeah, this one stings a bit for me.

This all feels backward, doesn't it? Our culture says power is domination, volume, and force. Scripture says it's ruling your spirit. Anyone can flex muscle or throw a tantrum. It takes far more strength to rule your emotions, your impulses, and your reactions. Meanwhile, God says, "Chill."

Think about how many disasters could've been avoided if someone had just paused long enough to breathe. How many arguments escalated only because nobody was willing to back down? How many poor choices were made in the heat of the moment that ended up haunting someone for years? Proverbs is clear: the mighty might win battles, but the wise win with self-control. #mindblown

Ruling your spirit doesn't mean stuffing your emotions or pretending they don't exist. It means learning to master them instead of letting them master you. Anger isn't in charge, *you* are. Fear doesn't call the shots, *God* does. Impulses don't get to run wild, *you* bring them under His authority. That's not weakness. That's strength!

Jesus modeled this perfectly. He had the power to call down angels at any moment. He had the authority to silence His accusers. Instead, He chose restraint. He ruled His spirit with perfect self-control because *His mission mattered more than proving a point.* That's what true strength looks like.

So maybe today's wisdom is this: don't measure your strength by how loudly you speak, how fast you react, or how hard you push. Measure it by how much control you're willing to surrender to God. The strongest person in the room isn't the one who wins the argument, it's the one who refuses to be ruled by their temper, their fear, or their pride.

Let's Reflect

- When has self-control saved you from a bad outcome? When could a situation have gone better if you or the other person had exhibited more restraint?
- Which is harder for you, holding your tongue or calming your emotions, and why?
- How could you practice keeping your spirit in check in your current season?

Let's Pray

Lord, I want to be strong in the ways that matter to You. Teach me to rule my spirit with wisdom instead of letting my emotions overtake my attitude and behavior. Help me to pause, breathe, and choose self-control when I'm tempted to react. Thank You for showing me through Jesus that *real* strength is restraint. Amen.

Bottom Line

If you can't rule yourself, you've got no business ruling anything else.

Day 18 – *Safe Tower*

Verse: Proverbs 18:10 – *The name of the Lord is a strong tower; the righteous man runs into it and is safe.*

Let's Dig In

When life falls apart, we all run somewhere. Some of us run to people. Some of us run to distractions. Some of us run to comfort food, retail therapy, or numbing out on our phones (*guilty*). Proverbs 18:10 reminds us where true safety is found: "The name of the Lord is a strong tower; the righteous man runs into it and is safe."

A tower in biblical times wasn't just a pretty building. It was protection. It was high, secure, and built to withstand attacks. That's the picture God gives us of His name, His character, His promises, His very presence. When trouble comes, His name is where we run for safety. He *is* our tower.

The question is, do we actually run to Him first? Or do we exhaust every other option and *then* call on God as a last resort? If we're brutally honest, it's usually the second one. We panic, scramble, and try to fix things ourselves. Seriously, how's that working out for you? Only when we smack into the wall do we say, "God, I need You."

This verse is an invitation to flip that around. Run to Him *first*. Run to Him *quickly*. His name is a strong tower; you don't have to wait until everything falls apart to seek His protection!

Safety doesn't mean life will suddenly be easy. It doesn't mean the storm disappears. It means you're covered. You're secure. You can rest because you know who's holding you. That's different from a false sense of security in temporary fixes that fade fast. God's safety is real, steady, and unshakable.

Think back on your own life. When have you felt God as your strong tower? Maybe it was in a crisis when His peace surrounded you in ways you couldn't explain. Maybe it was in grief when His presence was the only thing that kept you standing. Those moments remind us that safety isn't about perfect circumstances, it's about the unshakable, perfect presence of God.

So, here's today's challenge: notice where you've been running when trouble hits. If it hasn't been to Him, it's time to change course. His name is still the strong tower. The door is still open. All you have to do is run in!

Let's Reflect

- Where do you usually run first when life falls apart: panic, people, or prayer?
- How has God been your strong tower in the past?
- What would it look like for you to run to Him immediately instead of waiting until the last resort?

Let's Pray

Lord, when trouble comes, I admit that I often run to everything but You. Teach me to run to Your name first. Be my strong tower, the place I know I'm secure, no matter what storm I'm facing. Thank You that, in You, I can find safety that nothing in this world can take away. Amen.

Bottom Line

Stop running to Google before you run to God.

Day 19 – *Life or Death*

Verse: Proverbs 18:21 – *Death and life are in the power of the tongue, and those who love it will eat its fruits.*

Let's Dig In

Our words are *never* neutral. Every time we open our mouths, we're planting seeds, seeds that will either grow into life-giving fruit or into choking weeds (guess which often spews from *my* pie hole?). Proverbs 18:21 puts it bluntly: death and life are in the power of the tongue. That's a lot of power for something so small.

We've all seen this play out. A single encouragement can carry someone for weeks. A single insult can linger for years. Teachers, parents, friends, pastors, maybe even strangers, have spoken words to us that still echo in our heads today, for better or worse. Words don't just land and disappear; they take root.

This proverb also says we'll "eat its fruits." In other words, we don't just dish out the effects of our words on others; we live with the harvest they create in our own lives too. Harsh, thoughtless speech poisons the soil around us. It strains relationships, destroys trust, and leaves us surrounded by bitterness. Life-giving words, on the other hand, produce joy, peace, and encouragement, not only for others but for us as well (Not sure about that one? Try giving someone a compliment next time you're in a store. You'll be glad you did.)

That means every conversation is an opportunity. Every text, every post, every passing comment, each one has the potential to grow something. The question is, what are you planting? Are your words *feeding life* into your relationships, or are they *slowly starving* them?

This isn't about walking on eggshells or being fake. It's about being intentional. It's pausing before speaking and asking: will this build or will it break? Will this point to truth or just add more noise? Wisdom knows the difference. That's where God comes in (as if you didn't know where this was headed).

Jesus said in Matthew 12:36 that we'll give an account for every careless word. That's sobering! It means our words matter more than we often treat them. Yet it's also motivating because if careless words can wound, intentional words can heal. If death is an option, so is life.

So, here's today's challenge: plant words that you'll be glad to harvest. Speak encouragement into someone who needs it. Offer forgiveness instead of bitterness. Tell the truth in love instead of tearing down in anger. You'll eat the fruit either way, make sure it's worth tasting.

Let's Reflect

- What "crop" have your words been producing in your closest relationships?
- How could your words bring more life into your home, workplace, or friendships this week?
- Who needs a life-giving word from you today?

Let's Pray

Lord, thank You for reminding me that my words matter. Forgive me for the careless ones that have hurt others. Help me choose words that bring life instead of death. Teach me to plant seeds of encouragement, truth, and hope in every conversation. Thank You that You've spoken life over me so I can speak life into others. Amen.

Bottom Line

If you don't want to eat it, don't plant it.

Day 20 – *God's Plans Win*

Verse: Proverbs 19:21 – *Many are the plans in the mind of a man, but it is the purpose of the Lord that will stand.*

Let's Dig In

We're planners by default. We map out our weeks, sketch out our futures, and sometimes even try to script out how God should work in our lives. Proverbs 19:21 puts it in perspective: our plans may be many, but at the end of the day, it's God's purpose that stands. God doesn't need your color-coded planner, but thanks for sharing. (Case in point: my daughter had the most beautiful, color-coded spreadsheet of every minute detail of her wedding… and it rained… again, as I mentioned previously, my husband says, "Man plans, God laughs." Just so you know, her wedding ended up being the most amazing day I've ever experienced despite having the ceremony at the venue instead of the gorgeous cliff overlooking Montauk Point Lighthouse… whatever… the beauty of the day was not dependent on whether the sky was blue).

That can all feel frustrating, especially when our carefully crafted plans fall apart. You thought the job was perfect, but the door slammed shut. You thought the relationship was "the one," but it crumbled. You thought life would look a certain way by now, but it doesn't. It's tempting to see those detours as failures. This verse reminds us they're not, they're redirections. God's purpose is still on track, even when ours isn't.

Think about how exhausting it is to fight for your plans when God is directing you another path. It's like rowing upstream against a current. You can strain all you want, but you're not going to "out-muscle" the flow. God's purposes are the current, and they will keep moving with or without your cooperation. Wisdom is learning to turn the boat and go *with* Him instead of *against* Him.

This doesn't mean planning is pointless. God gave us minds, creativity, and responsibility. The danger comes when we start treating *our* plans as unshakable. Plans are pencil. God's purposes are Sharpie®. When we hold our plans loosely, we leave space for Him to shape them into something better than we imagined.

Most of us can look back and thank God for *not* giving us what we once begged for. At the time, it felt like disappointment. Later, we realized it was protection. He saw what we couldn't, and His purpose was better than our plan. That's what this verse calls us to remember in the moment: God's purposes are trustworthy, even when they don't match our script (2nd case in point: daughter #2 didn't get accepted to the college she had hoped for… in the end it was a blessing).

So, here's today's wisdom: make your plans, but hand them over. Set goals, but stay open. Trust that the only plans guaranteed to last are His. That's not a threat, it's a promise.

Let's Reflect

- When has God's purpose overridden your plans in a way that turned out better than you expected?
- How can you start holding your current plans more loosely?

- What does trusting God's purpose look like in your life right now?

Let's Pray

God, I confess that I like to cling to my plans. It feels safer to think I'm in control. Help me to remember that *Your* purpose is the one that stands, not mine. Give me the humility to let You redirect me and the faith to trust that Your way is always better. Thank You for being faithful even when my plans fail. Amen.

Bottom Line

Your plans are in pencil. God's will is in pen.

Day 21 – *Legacy Check*

Verse: Proverbs 20:7 – *The righteous who walks in his integrity; blessed are his children after him!*

Let's Dig In

Integrity isn't just about you. It's about the trail you're leaving behind (oof!). Proverbs 20:7 reminds us that when someone walks in righteousness and integrity, the blessing doesn't stop with them, it flows to their children and beyond. Your life is shaping a legacy, whether you realize it or not. Think back a few days to the bit about planting seeds; are your seeds growing yummy fruits, or are they spreading deadly weeds to choke out the good stuff?

We live in a world that applauds quick wins and short-term gains. Integrity doesn't always look impressive at the start. Sometimes it means walking away from opportunities that would benefit you in that moment but compromise your values in the end. Sometimes it means telling the truth when a lie would be easier. Sometimes it means staying faithful in small, hidden things when nobody's watching. Those choices don't always make headlines, but they build something lasting.

The opposite is true, too. A life of compromise leaves wreckage, broken trust, and shaky foundations, even generations that carry the consequences of poor choices. Scripture is blunt: your integrity (or lack of it) doesn't just affect you, it ripples outward.

This isn't meant to heap guilt but to remind us of the opportunity we have. Every choice is a brick in the legacy we're building (sick metaphor, right?). Are you stacking bricks of honesty, faithfulness, and integrity? Or are you cutting corners that will crumble later?

Integrity doesn't mean perfection. Nobody gets it right every time. It means consistency. *It means living in such a way that who you are in private matches who you are in public.* It means admitting when you're wrong instead of covering it up. It means choosing the long game of character over the short game of convenience.

Think about the people who've influenced your faith the most. Chances are, it wasn't their charm, talent, or success that left the mark. It was their integrity. Their steady walk with God. Their honesty. Their consistency. That's the kind of life Proverbs says blesses not just you, but the generations *after* you.

So, here's today's challenge: take a legacy check. What kind of trail are you leaving behind? What kind of inheritance are you building for the people who will come after you? The righteous walk may not always feel glamorous, but it's the kind of life that leaves blessings long after you're gone. Again: #micdrop

Let's Reflect

- What kind of legacy are you building right now with your words, actions, and habits?
- How has someone else's integrity shaped your life for the better?
- What's one way you could live more consistently this week so others see God in you?

Let's Pray

Lord, thank You for reminding me that my life is bigger than just me. Help me to walk in integrity in the little things and the big things. Give me the courage to choose honesty, consistency, and righteousness even when it's hard. Let my life be a blessing to those who come after me, pointing them to You long after I'm gone. Amen.

Bottom Line

Your legacy starts with your next choice.

WEEK 4 – Strength in the Storm

Life's storms may rock you, but wisdom will anchor you.

Day 22 – *Let God Handle It*

Verse: Proverbs 20:22 – *Do not say, "I will repay evil"; wait for the Lord, and he will deliver you.*

Let's Dig In

Revenge feels satisfying in the moment. Someone wrongs you, and your first instinct is to make sure they feel it back. Look, my halo is crooked on a *good* day; I might not intend to plot a full-blown movie-style revenge, but I often imagine the perfect comeback, the way I'd expose them, or how I'd make them regret messing with me (often and sadly, after the moment has passed). Are you with me on this? It feels good in your head, but Proverbs 20:22 reminds us it's not our job. *"Do not say, 'I will repay evil'; wait for the Lord, and he will deliver you."*

The truth is, revenge never works the way we think it will. Even if you "win" the moment, it rarely satisfies for long. Usually it just makes the wound deeper, the conflict messier, and the bitterness stronger. That's because you and I were never designed to be the judge. God didn't hand us the gavel. He reserved that role for Himself because He alone knows the full story. He sees motives we can't and the behind-the-scenes details we'll never know. He judges with perfect justice.

Waiting on Him doesn't make you weak, it makes you *wise*. It means you trust God to handle what only *He* can handle. It doesn't excuse the wrong that was done, but it keeps you from becoming just like the person who hurt you. Revenge pulls you down to their level; trust lifts you into God's care. Let's not sugarcoat it, you know *exactly* what I mean. I've given friends that same advice, haven't you? Funny how we preach but don't practice what we say to others, huh?

Think about how much peace you've lost stewing over someone else's offense. The conversations you've replayed in your head. The imaginary arguments you've had in the shower. The time you've wasted plotting a comeback. None of it actually fixes the situation! All it does is drain you and you know that! Handing it to God *frees* you. It puts the weight back where it belongs: on the shoulders of the *only* One who can carry it.

Letting God handle it doesn't mean sitting back and doing nothing if boundaries are needed. It doesn't mean you allow abuse or stay silent in the face of injustice. What it means is you choose not to take matters into your own hands for payback. You set boundaries, you speak truth, but you leave the score-settling to Him. Holy boundaries > hot mess situations.

Jesus modeled this perfectly (anyone know how many times I've said that already in this book?). When He was insulted, accused, and beaten, He didn't fight back or call down armies of angels. He entrusted Himself to the Father, knowing ultimate justice would come. If the Son of God could trust His Father with injustice *that severe*, we can trust Him with the wrongs in our own lives, too.

So, here's today's challenge: stop wasting your energy plotting revenge. Start handing over the gavel! Trust that God's justice is *always* fair and His timing is *always* right. He doesn't need your help settling the score.

Let's Reflect

- When have you tried to get even and just made things worse?
- What does "waiting for the Lord" look like in your current situation?
- How could trusting God's justice bring you more peace?

Let's Pray

Lord, You *know* how much I want to fight back when I'm wronged. Help me to trust Your justice and keep my hands off the gavel. Teach me to set healthy boundaries without seeking payback. Thank You for promising that You see it *all* and that You will deliver me in Your perfect way. Amen.

Bottom Line

Vengeance is the Lord's. He doesn't need your help.

Day 23 – *Mouth Insurance*

Verse: Proverbs 21:23 – *Whoever keeps his mouth and his tongue keeps himself out of trouble.*

Let's Dig In

Friends, how many days do we have to devote to this? Answer: never enough. This one, however, is straight to the point: fewer words, fewer problems. Proverbs 21:23 is basically saying, "Want less drama in your life? Guard your mouth." It's not rocket science, but it is wisdom most of us ignore far too often. I mean, come on, how many days of this theme are we up to already?

We all know what it feels like to wish we could take words back. Maybe it was something said in anger. Maybe it was gossip that slipped out. Maybe it was sarcasm that went too far. The words felt small in the moment, but they carried consequences that stuck around long after. That's the trouble Proverbs is talking about, the kind we bring on ourselves with careless speech. Are you seeing a trend here?

Guarding your mouth is like buying insurance. You pay attention up front so you don't deal with disaster later. A pause before speaking is usually cheaper than an apology after (and don't I know it). A moment of restraint can save a relationship, a reputation, or even your witness.

This doesn't mean *never* speaking up. It doesn't mean bottling everything inside until you explode. It means weighing your words before you release them. It means asking: will this help or hurt? Is it necessary or just noise? Is it true, or am I exaggerating? The extra second it takes to ask those questions is often the difference between peace and regret.

Most of us underestimate the power of our tongues. We treat words like throwaways, but Scripture is clear: words build or break, bless or curse, protect or wound. *Guarding your mouth is a discipline that shows wisdom, maturity, and humility.* It says, "I don't need to say everything I think. I don't need to join every conversation. I don't need to win every argument."

Here's a bonus: it's not just you who benefits. When you guard your mouth, you protect the people around you, too. Your spouse, your kids, your coworkers, your friends, they all live with the ripple effects of your words. Self-control in your speech creates safety for everyone in your circle.

So, maybe today's wisdom is simple: think of your mouth like a door. Not everything inside needs to come out. Lock it when necessary, open it with prudence, and you'll save yourself from a bunch of self-inflicted trouble.

Let's Reflect

- When have your words landed you in trouble?

- What's one practical way to guard your speech this week?

- Who benefits when you practice restraint?

Let's Pray

God, I know how quickly my words can get me into trouble. Teach me to guard my mouth with wisdom and self-control. Help me to slow down, think, and pray before I speak. Let my words be careful, thoughtful, and filled with life. Thank You for reminding me that silence at the right time can be just as powerful as speech. Amen.

Bottom Line

Your tongue can write checks that your life can't cash.

Day 24 – *The Long Game*

Verse: Proverbs 22:6 – *Train up a child in the way he should go; even when he is old he will not depart from it.*

Let's Dig In

Raising kids (or mentoring anyone, really) isn't for the faint of heart. You're in for the long game. There are no instant results, no immediate guarantees, and no "one-size-fits-all" formulas. Proverbs 22:6 reminds us that the seeds we plant today may not sprout for years, but that doesn't mean they aren't growing beneath the surface.

This verse is often quoted by parents with equal parts hope and desperation (oof, facts). We want to believe that if we raise our kids in the right way, they'll never wander. Yet Proverbs is a book of wisdom, not ironclad promises. The principle here is that what you plant matters. We discussed that earlier. The way you train, model, and shape a child, or anyone God has placed in your care, leaves a mark that doesn't easily fade.

The challenge is patience. Training is daily work. It's not glamorous. It's not quick. It's repeating the same truth over and over, modeling godly behavior when no one seems to notice, and trusting that God is at work even when you can't see results. Seeds don't grow overnight. They need time, sunlight, water, and a lot of waiting. Faithful training works the same way.

Maybe you've been sowing into your kids, your students, or someone you're mentoring, and you're not seeing the fruit yet. Don't give up! Wisdom is reminding you that *the investment is worth it*! The lessons you teach, the prayers you pray, the example you set, they're all adding up, even if it feels invisible right now. God sees every seed you sow, and He knows how and when they'll sprout.

It's also worth remembering that training isn't just about words. Kids (really *anyone* you're leading) are watching how you live. They're learning as much from your habits, your priorities, and your character as they are from your lectures. Living the truth in front of them is training too. Integrity speaks louder than instruction.

So, here's today's encouragement: don't measure success by immediate results. Measure it by *faithfulness*. Keep planting, keep modeling, keep praying. Trust God with the harvest. You may not see all the fruit in *your* lifetime, but His Word assures us that seeds sown in faith will not be wasted. Take that to the bank.

Let's Reflect

- Who has God placed in your life to disciple or mentor?

- How have you seen seeds of truth take root over time?

- What's one intentional way you can model godliness this week?

Let's Pray

Lord, thank You for the opportunity to invest in the next generation. Help me to stay patient and faithful when I can't see results yet.

Remind me that every prayer, every word of truth, and every act of faithfulness matters. Give me wisdom to model integrity and faith in a way that points others to You. Amen.

Bottom Line

You're sowing, not microwaving. There's no shortcut, just faith.

Day 25 – *Check Your Company*

Verse: Proverbs 22:24–25 – *Make no friendship with a man given to anger… lest you learn his ways and entangle yourself in a snare.*

Let's Dig In

Anger is contagious. Spend enough time with someone whose temper runs hot, and yours will, too. Proverbs warns us that our circle shapes our spirit, for better or worse. Walk with someone whose default setting is wrath, and you'll pick up the habits, the tone, and the fallout. It's not just about avoiding drama, it's about *protecting your soul*. That hit hard, didn't it?

We like to think we're immune to other people's influence. "I can hang out with them without being like them." Truth is, that's rarely how it works. The people closest to us rub off on us. Their values, their speech, and their reactions seep into ours. Slowly, without even realizing it, you start mirroring what you're around. Oh, the receipts I could produce.

That's why Scripture calls us to check our company. It doesn't mean we isolate ourselves or avoid every imperfect person; we'd all fail that test. It *does* mean we pay attention to who we're letting into our inner circle. The people who get your time, your trust, and your heart are the people who shape you most. If their anger, bitterness, or foolishness goes unchecked, you're not just watching it, you're absorbing it.

Think of it like secondhand smoke. You don't have to light up to feel the effects. Breathing it in long enough still hurts you. In the same way, being around constant anger entangles you in snares that aren't even yours. Suddenly you're more irritable, more defensive, quicker to snap. That's the influence Proverbs is warning us against.

On the flip side, the right company can shape you for the better! Walk with patient people, and you'll learn patience. Surround yourself with encouragers, and you'll naturally start encouraging. Spend time with people who chase after God, and your faith will grow stronger. *Your vibe really does attract your tribe, and vice versa.*

So, here's today's wisdom: take a hard look at your circle. Who stirs up your worst traits, and who pulls out your best? Who helps you walk closer with God, and who drags you further away? Wisdom means setting boundaries where you need to, even if it's uncomfortable. Your spiritual health depends on it.

Let's Reflect

- Who in your circle stirs up your worst traits?

- How have you been shaped by someone's good example?

- What boundaries do you need to set for your own spiritual health?

Let's Pray

God, thank You for the gift of community and friendship. Show me clearly which people are helping me grow closer to You and which ones are pulling me away. Give me courage to set healthy boundaries where I need to, and surround me with people who reflect Your wisdom, patience, and grace. Amen.

Bottom Line

Your vibe attracts your tribe, and vice versa.

Day 26 – *Get Back Up*

Verse: Proverbs 24:16 – *For the righteous falls seven times and rises again, but the wicked stumble in times of calamity.*

Let's Dig In

Everybody falls. That's not the question. The question is whether you'll get back up. Proverbs 24:16 says even the righteous stumble, not once, not twice, but *seven times*. The difference is that they rise again. Falling isn't failure. Staying down is. I'm sure you've heard that advice: if you fall down seven times, get up eight. Cute, right? Yeah, it's actually Biblical.

We tend to think of righteousness as perfection. This verse shatters that delusion (I originally wrote "illusion" but "delusion" is a better fit). Righteous people still trip, they still mess up and still face setbacks. What makes them different is their response. They don't stay flat on the ground. They rise again because their strength isn't rooted in themselves, it's *rooted in God*!

The wicked stumble too, but they don't recover. Without God's grace and power, there's nothing to pull them back up. That's the contrast Proverbs is attempting to make clear. Falling with God means resilience, getting back up, learning, growing. Falling without Him means collapse, defeat, and ultimately, staying down.

Think about your own story. How many times have you been knocked down, by heartbreak, failure, disappointment, or sin, and thought, "This is it, I'm done"? Yet here you are, still standing. That's proof of God's mercy in your life. His grace picked you up when you couldn't do it on your own. We can never do it on our own, you know.

Getting back up doesn't mean ignoring the fall. It doesn't erase the pain or undo the consequences of what happened. It means you refuse to allow the fall to have the final word. It means accepting forgiveness, learning from the fall, and moving forward with God's strength. That's what separates resilience from despair.

Every stumble is also an opportunity. It's a moment to discover the depth of God's grace in a fresh way. His mercies are new every morning, which means *no fall has to define you*. His hand is always extended out to help lift you up again.

So, if you're down right now, hear this: you don't have to stay there. God isn't finished with you! Stand up. Dust off. Lean into His strength. Falling doesn't define your story, but rising does!

Let's Reflect

- When have you been tempted to strut in righteousness only to be shut down?

- Where are you tempted to stay down instead of standing back up?

- How can you remind yourself daily that His mercy is greater than your failures and His hand is always reaching out to lift you up?

Let's Pray

Lord, thank You that stumbling doesn't end my story. Thank You for the grace that picks me up every time I fall. Give me the courage to rise again and the humility to lean on You instead of my own strength. Remind me that Your mercy is greater than my mistakes. Amen.

Bottom Line

Falling isn't failure. Staying down is.

Day 27 – *No Gloating*

Verse: Proverbs 24:17-18 – *Do not rejoice when your enemy falls, and let not your heart be glad when he stumbles, lest the Lord see it and be displeased, and turn away his anger from him.*

Let's Dig In

It's human nature to want payback. When someone who hurt you stumbles, there's a part of you that wants to say, "Good, serves them right." Proverbs 24:17–18 stops us in our tracks. God says, don't rejoice when your enemy falls. Don't clap, don't smirk, don't celebrate. (If conviction burned calories, I'd be a size 2.)

That feels unnatural, doesn't it? Especially when we feel the person deserves it. Yet here's the thing: God takes our gloating seriously. The verse even says He may ease up on judging them if He sees us gloating over it. Why? Gloating reveals a *heart problem*. It means we're craving vengeance instead of trusting *God's justice*.

Here's the danger: when you gloat, you start to look just like the person who hurt you. The bitterness that drove them to wound you starts taking root in *you*. Before long, you're pouring the very poison you wanted *them* to drink.

Choosing not to rejoice in someone else's downfall doesn't mean you excuse what they did. It doesn't mean you pretend it didn't hurt. It means you trust God enough to handle justice His way, in

His timing. You don't need to sit in the judge's seat, He's already there.

Think about it: what do you gain by gloating? Does it heal the wound? Does it bring peace? No. It might feel good for five minutes, but afterward you're still carrying the same weight of resentment. Refusing to gloat, on the other hand, keeps your heart clean. It frees you from feeding the cycle of bitterness.

Jesus modeled this perfectly. On the cross, He didn't gloat over His enemies. He prayed for them. He trusted His Father with the justice part. That's strength, and it's the kind of strength Proverbs is calling us to.

So, here's today's challenge: check your heart when someone who hurt you faces consequences. Instead of celebrating, pray. Instead of smirking, release it. Let God be the judge and let Him protect your heart keep it from turning hard in the process.

Let's Reflect

- When have you been tempted to gloat over someone else's downfall?

- How does trusting God's justice free you from that temptation?

- What's one practical way you can respond differently the next time you feel like celebrating someone else's stumble?

Let's Pray

Lord, You know how tempting it is to feel satisfied when someone who hurt me falls. Guard my heart from gloating. Teach me to trust Your justice instead of craving revenge. Keep my spirit soft and free from bitterness. Thank You for being a righteous Judge who sees it all. Amen.

Bottom Line

Schadenfreude isn't a fruit of the Spirit. Gloating over someone else's fall makes you trip, too.

Day 28 – *Future Focused*

Verse: Proverbs 24:19-20 – *Fret not yourself because of evildoers, and be not envious of the wicked, for the evil man has no future; the lamp of the wicked will be put out.*

Let's Dig In

It's easy to look around and question why people who cut corners often seem to get ahead. The coworker who lies gets promoted. The neighbor who cheats looks like they're thriving. The person who hurt you seems to live without consequences. If you've ever thought, "Why do they have it so good while I'm over here struggling to do the right thing?", you're not alone. Proverbs 24:19–20 speaks directly to that frustration: don't fret, and don't envy. Their success isn't built to last.

When you fixate on evildoers, two things happen: you either get discouraged or you get envious. Discouraged, because it feels like doing the right thing doesn't matter. Envious, because you start wishing you could cut corners too. Both are traps. Both shift your focus from God's promises to someone else's temporary wins.

Proverbs reminds us: the wicked have no future. Whatever looks shiny now is fading. Their lamp will be snuffed. It may not happen on *your* timeline, but God's justice is certain. You don't need to obsess over *their* story, you need to stay faithful in *yours*.

This isn't just about "bad people out there." It's about our own hearts, too. How often do we slip into comparing our lives with others and resenting God's timing or provisions? Wisdom calls us back to trust. God sees the full picture. He knows the end from the beginning. He promises that the path of the righteous shines brighter and brighter (Proverbs 4:18). Your lamp won't burn out because it's fueled by Him.

So, instead of fretting over the wicked, focus on your future in Christ. Instead of comparing, trust the One who holds your story. Their lamp may flicker out, but yours is being tended by the eternal Light of the world. *mic drop #2*

Let's Reflect

- When have you been tempted to envy people who don't follow God?

- How does remembering their "no future" change your perspective?

- What's one practical way you can stay focused on your path instead of comparing?

Let's Pray

Lord, forgive me for the times I've envied people who seem to prosper while ignoring You. Help me trust that their success is temporary, but Your promises are eternal. Keep my eyes on You and my hope fixed on the future that You've secured for me. Thank You that my lamp won't burn out because *You* are my light. Amen.

Bottom Line

Don't waste today envying what won't exist tomorrow.

WEEK 5 – Living with Purpose

Purpose shows in the life you live,
not the credit you take.

Day 29 – *The Power of Soft*

Verse: Proverbs 25:15 – *With patience a ruler may be persuaded, and a soft tongue will break a bone.*

_____

Let's Dig In

A soft tongue can break bones? Say what now? I seriously don't get that. First of all, I wouldn't consider myself to EVER have had an issue with that! (Hush, don't judge). Needless to say, when I came upon this Proverb I knew I needed to research it deeper. We tend to think loud voices and hard stances equal strength, while patience and softness look like being a pushover. Proverbs flips that idea. It says patience *can* persuade rulers, and gentleness *can* break bones. In other words, quiet strength often accomplishes more than force ever could. (Ahhh, that explains a lot)

Think about the last time someone spoke harshly to you. What was your immediate reaction? Probably to get defensive, maybe to shut down, or to fight back. Now think of the last time someone corrected you or challenged you with gentleness. You may not have liked it in the moment, but you were more likely to actually hear it. That's the power of soft, it disarms instead of provokes.

This verse isn't telling us to be passive. It's showing us the effectiveness of *controlled strength*. Anyone can shout. Anyone can steamroll. It takes real wisdom and maturity to respond with calm, patience, and gentleness, especially when everything in you wants to come in hot, swinging and spewing not-nice things.

Jesus lived this perfectly (I know, I know… I say that all the time. That's the point, isn't it?) Jesus wasn't weak. He flipped tables when needed, spoke truth to power, and called out hypocrisy without flinching. Yet when He dealt with the broken, the hurting, or even His disciples who *constantly* misunderstood Him, He was patient and gentle. His "soft tongue" didn't compromise truth, it delivered it in a way that could *actually be received*.

Gentleness isn't about diluting the message. It's about strengthening the delivery (oof, another truth bomb!). A whisper can carry more weight than a shout when it comes from a heart rooted in wisdom. Softness may not feel powerful, but Proverbs says it's the kind of power that lasts.

So, here's today's challenge: don't underestimate gentleness. Try patience before pushing. Try softness before force. It may just be the very thing that breaks through where your hammer never could.

Let's Reflect

- Who in your life responds better to gentle persuasion than to force?

- How has patience won you a bigger victory than aggression?

- Where do you need to swap your hammer for a feather?

Let's Pray

God, teach me the strength of gentleness and the power of patience. Help me resist the urge to push harder when what's needed is a softer word. Shape my tone so it reflects Your wisdom and makes room for peace instead of strife. Thank You that true power is found in self-control, not force (because, Lord, You know I need Your help with this). Amen.

Bottom Line

Sometimes the whisper wins the war.

Day 30 – *Tomorrow's Not Yours*

Verse: Proverbs 27:1 – *Do not boast about tomorrow, for you do not know what a day may bring.*

Let's Dig In

We live like tomorrow is guaranteed. We make plans, book calendars months out, and assume there will always be more time to get around to the important stuff. I admit, I'm a planner. I love my calendar app. I love my notes app and sticky notes. I am punctual and prepared because that's the way my momma raised me! Proverbs 27:1 reminds us how fragile that thinking is: you don't know what a day may bring. Tomorrow isn't promised.

That's not meant to make you panic. It's meant to shift your priorities. If something matters, don't wait. If someone needs encouragement, don't delay. If God has placed a calling on your heart, stop putting it off until "someday." Someday isn't real, it's just another word for never. Does that mean I should abandon using a calendar and jotting reminders on my cellphone? Let's not go crazy, those things definitely have their place in life. However, does your Google® Calendar hold the key to your happiness in life?

Think about how much procrastination costs us spiritually. We assume we'll pray more tomorrow, serve more tomorrow, reconcile tomorrow, obey tomorrow. Then tomorrow gets busy, or stressful, or simply never comes. Before we know it, opportunities slip by.

People move on. Words that needed to be said remain unsaid. The laundry will get folded (I had to include that).

This verse is a call to urgency, but also to humility. We don't control the future. We don't control the next 24 hours or even the next 20 minutes. Only God does. Acknowledging that doesn't mean living recklessly, it means living faithfully, living purposefully. It means asking, "What has God given me to do today, and how can I bring honor to Him by being faithful in it?"

Jesus taught the same truth when He said, *"Do not worry about tomorrow, for tomorrow will worry about itself"* (Matthew 6:34). Worrying about the future won't change it. Boasting about it won't guarantee it. All we have is today, and that's more than enough when we put it in His hands.

So, here's today's challenge: stop living like tomorrow is a sure thing. Start living like today is the gift it really is. Speak the words. Show the love. Do the thing. You don't know what tomorrow will bring, but you know Who holds it. That's enough. (Pay your bills, though… God provides us with utilities to live comfortably, but He doesn't pay the bill.)

Let's Reflect

- What's something you've been putting off that God's calling you to do *today*?

- How would living with urgency change your priorities?

- What's one way you can honor God in the next 24 hours?

Let's Pray

Lord, teach me to number my days and live like each one matters. Keep me from wasting today by assuming I'll always have tomorrow. Give me urgency to obey, to encourage, and to live faithfully with the time You've given me. Thank You for being the God of every day: past, present, and future. Amen.

Bottom Line

Tomorrow is a rumor, not a promise.

Day 31 – *Let Others Say It*

Verse: Proverbs 27:2 – *Let another praise you, and not your own mouth; a stranger, and not your own lips.*

Let's Dig In

We live in a world that rewards self-promotion. Post your accomplishments, highlight your strengths, sell yourself to get noticed. Fill your social media feed with how well things are going for you: the new car you treated yourself to, your recent shopping haul, your daily selfies, and every time you step into the gym. The louder you shout, the more people seem to listen, right? Proverbs 27:2 cuts right through that noise: don't praise yourself. Let someone else do it.

There's something refreshing about humility. It doesn't need a spotlight, yet it stands out. A person with integrity doesn't have to announce how great they are, their actions speak for them. People notice. God notices. When praise comes, it carries more weight because it wasn't demanded.

On the flip side, self-promotion usually backfires. The more you talk yourself up, the less people believe you. It's like laughing at your own joke, it takes the power out of it. Real respect is earned, not advertised. Be honest: who popped into your head just now?

This isn't about pretending you're worthless or ignoring your gifts. It's about perspective. Every talent, every achievement, every opportunity comes from God. He's the source. So, if there's any boasting to be done, let it be about Him. Paul said it this way in 1 Corinthians 1:31: "Let the one who boasts, boast in the Lord."

Think of the people you admire most. Odds are, it's not the loud bragger. It's the one who consistently lives with integrity, serves quietly, and lets their life, not their lips, do the talking. That's the kind of life Proverbs is pointing us toward. Case in point: my daughter, the dancer, never brags about her talent. This doesn't necessarily mean that she believes she's not good, but she *does* believe that her talent is God-given, so, she works at it to the best of her ability in an effort to honor and glorify Him. I wish I had that level of humility and integrity.

So, here's today's wisdom: stop trying to write your own headlines. Let humility be your reputation. If there's something worth praising, let it come from others, and ultimately, let all the praise roll back to God!

Let's Reflect

- When have you been tempted to brag about yourself?

- How does humility make your witness stronger?

- What's one quiet act of service you could do this week without seeking recognition?

Let's Pray

Lord, help me live in such a way that I don't need to promote myself. Let my life speak louder than my mouth ever could. Remind me that everything I have is from You, and that all praise belongs back in Your hands. Amen.

Bottom Line

If you have to say you're great, you're probably not.

Day 32 – *Bold as a Lion*

Verse: Proverbs 28:1 – *The wicked flee when no one pursues, but the righteous are bold as a lion.*

Let's Dig In

Fear makes people run even when no one is chasing them. Guilt, shame, and compromise keep you looking over your shoulder, waiting for the other shoe to drop. That's the picture Proverbs gives us of the wicked: they live jumpy, paranoid, and unsure.

The righteous, on the other hand, are bold as a lion. Not cocky, not arrogant, but bold. Why? Look, when you're walking with God, you don't have to fear shadows. You don't have to flinch at every sound. You're standing on the right side, and that gives a confidence the world can't touch.

Boldness isn't about personality. You can be quiet and still be bold. You can be naturally shy and still carry "holy confidence". Boldness comes from knowing Who you belong to, what He's done for you, and where your security lies. When your conscience is clear and your trust is in the Lord, you don't waste energy running from the scary stuff in life.

Think about a lion. It's not creeping around the savanna stressing about who's watching. A lion doesn't need to prove itself, it just is. Bold, steady, unbothered. That's the kind of boldness Proverbs is talking about. Not cocky, not reckless, just quiet confidence because you know exactly Who you belong to.

This doesn't mean life will always feel safe or easy. Boldness doesn't remove obstacles; *it helps you face them.* It's standing firm when the culture shifts. It's speaking truth when silence would be easier. It's choosing faith over fear, again and again and again.

So, here's today's challenge: check where fear has been calling the shots in your life. Replace it with the boldness that comes from righteousness, not your own, but Christ's. You don't need to run from shadows. You can stand like a lion because your security is in Him.

Let's Reflect

- Where do you need holy boldness right now?

- How does righteousness give you courage?

- What's one fear you can hand over to God today?

Let's Pray

God, make me bold enough to stand for truth and humble enough to remember where my courage comes from. Teach me to walk in Your righteousness with confidence, not fear. Thank You that I don't have to run from shadows because I belong to You. Amen.

Bottom Line

Boldness is loudest when it's backed by righteousness.

Day 33 – *Mercy Wins*

Verse: Proverbs 28:13 – *Whoever conceals his transgressions will not prosper, but he who confesses and forsakes them will obtain mercy.*

Let's Dig In

We're all pretty good at cover-ups. We downplay our mistakes, excuse our sin, or hide parts of our story we'd rather no one know about. It feels safer that way, doesn't it? If people don't see the cracks, they can't judge us. Proverbs 28:13 says the opposite: concealing sin never leads to prosperity. The mold just keeps spreading under the fresh coat of paint. Big yuck.

Confession, though messy and uncomfortable, is where healing begins. Bringing sin into the light feels terrifying, but it's the only way to break free. When you confess and forsake sin, Proverbs promises mercy. Not shame. Not exile. Mercy.

That's because God already knows. You're not surprising Him when you confess, you're agreeing with Him. You're saying, "You're right, Lord. I need You here." In that humility, grace rushes in. Covering sin keeps you trapped; confessing sin sets you free.

Notice the verse doesn't stop with confession. It also says *forsake*. Confession without repentance is just admitting guilt without change. Mercy flows when you not only bring sin into the light but also turn away from it with God's help. That's where freedom starts.

We've all felt the weight of hiding. The anxiety of being found out. The energy it takes to keep the mask in place. Compare that to the peace of forgiveness, the relief of honesty, and the strength that comes from walking in the open. One is a prison. The other is freedom.

So, here's today's challenge: stop painting over mold. Bring it into the light. Let confession be the doorway to mercy and the first step toward a clean slate. God isn't waiting to shame you; He's waiting to forgive you. Again, He already knows; just go to him admitting that you do, too, and that you need Him to help set you free.

Let's Reflect

- What's something you've been trying to hide from God (or from others)?

- How have you experienced mercy after confession in the past?

- Why is forsaking sin (repenting and turning away from it) just as important as confessing it?

Let's Pray

Lord, give me the courage to bring my sin into the light and the strength to walk away from it. Thank You that mercy is waiting when I confess and forsake what holds me back. Help me trade the weight of hiding for the freedom of honesty. Amen.

Bottom Line

You can't heal what you won't reveal.

Day 34 – *Clothed in Strength*

Verse: Proverbs 31:25 – *Strength and dignity are her clothing, and she laughs at the time to come.*

Let's Dig In

This verse is often connected to the famous Proverbs 31 woman, but the wisdom here applies to every one of us. Strength and dignity aren't limited to a certain gender or role, they are garments God offers to all who trust Him. These are coverings that never fade, never go out of style, and never fail when life gets messy.

The world constantly tells us to clothe ourselves in image: success, wealth, popularity, appearance, all the things that look impressive on the outside. Yet those things wear thin fast. Proverbs points us toward what actually lasts: strength that anchors you when the storms come, and dignity that keeps your head up when compromise would be easier. When those are what you're "wearing," you are truly prepared for anything.

Look at the result: "she laughs at the time to come." That's not naïve optimism, it's confidence rooted in God. It means you can face the future without being paralyzed by fear, because your life is wrapped in something stronger than circumstances. You're covered in qualities that outlast layoffs, disappointments, sickness, or uncertainty. Strength keeps you steady; dignity keeps you grounded. Together, they free you to face tomorrow with joy instead of dread.

Think about it: what are you wearing spiritually right now? Maybe it's worry, insecurity, bitterness, or self-reliance. Those coverings feel heavy and leave you anxious about what's ahead. Or maybe you've experienced seasons when you've truly known God's strength covering your weakness, and His dignity guiding your choices. The difference is night and day, not just for you, but for the people around you who see how you carry yourself. I'm not wrong, am I?

This isn't about putting on a show. Clothing is what people see first, but it's also what protects you. When you let God clothe you in His strength and dignity, you're shielded against fear, against compromise, and against the temptation to define yourself by what fades. Others may notice, yes, but the real blessing is how it equips you to walk forward with confidence in Him.

Here's today's wisdom: stop settling for temporary coverings. Don't dress yourself in what culture says matters most. Those things unravel quickly. Jesus didn't die so you could live bitter and cranky. Instead, let God cover you in what truly endures. Strength and dignity aren't earned, they're *received* from Him. When you're wrapped in those, you can smile at the future instead of fearing it.

Let's Reflect

- What are you "wearing" spiritually right now? Fear, worry, or God's strength and dignity?

- How has God clothed you with strength in hard times?

- What's one way you can choose dignity in your daily choices this week?

Let's Pray

Lord, clothe me with the things that last. Cover me in Your strength so I can stand firm, and Your dignity so I can walk with integrity. Keep me from wrapping myself in what fades, and remind me that my confidence comes from You alone. Thank You, that when I'm covered in You, I can face the future without fear. Amen.

Bottom Line

Forget designer labels, wear what God gives you.

Day 35 – *Praise Where It's Due*

Verse: Proverbs 31:30 – *Charm is deceitful, and beauty is vain, but a woman who fears the Lord is to be praised.*

Let's Dig In

We live in a world obsessed with charm and beauty. Social media thrives on edited selfies, quick wit, and surface-level appeal, daily gym visits. None of that is new, Proverbs 31:30 calls it out plainly: charm deceives, beauty fades. What looks impressive now won't last. What endures is a heart anchored in reverence for the Lord. (I love how those words sound: *a heart anchored in reverence for the Lord.* Wow)

While this verse points to the Proverbs 31 woman, the principle stretches to *every* person. Charm and beauty, brains and brawn, whether it's how you look, how smooth you talk, or how well you play the part, are temporary. They can even be misleading. What really matters, what *really* deserves praise, is a life shaped by the fear of the Lord (remember what we discussed right from Day 1). That kind of character outlives physical appearance and outshines surface-level charisma.

Think about the people you truly admire. Odds are, it's not because of their looks or charm. It's because of their faith, their integrity, their kindness, their consistency. They've lived in such a way that even when trends change and seasons shift, their legacy points to God. That's the kind of praise Proverbs says is worth giving.

Notice this: the verse doesn't forbid admiration of beauty or appreciation of personality. It simply puts them in their proper place. They're not the foundation of worth. They're not what lasts. The fear of the Lord, the deep reverence that shapes decisions, attitudes, and relationships, are what carry eternal weight.

It's a reminder, too, about what kind of legacy we're chasing. If we spend our lives trying to stay charming or beautiful in the world's eyes, we'll end up exhausted and empty. If we spend our lives fearing the Lord, loving Him, honoring Him, and walking in His wisdom, we'll leave behind something that time and culture can't erase. That's true praise. That's a life well lived.

Here's today's challenge: check what you're chasing. Are you building your worth on things that fade, or are you cultivating a fear of the Lord that grows richer over time? One brings temporary applause. The other brings eternal reward.

Let's Reflect

- What qualities do you most admire in a godly person?

- How can you cultivate the fear of the Lord in your daily choices?

- What kind of legacy do you want to leave behind?

Let's Pray

Lord, keep me from chasing what fades. Teach me to build my life on what matters most: fearing You, honoring You, and living for Your glory. Let my character outshine any charm or beauty this world values. May my life be one that points to You and leaves behind a legacy worth praising because it reflects You. Amen.

Bottom Line

Beauty fades. Godly stays.

WEEK 6 – Wisdom in Action

Living it out in real choices, work, and daily life.

Day 36 – *Diligence Pays Off*

Verse: Proverbs 12:24 – *The hand of the diligent will rule, while the slothful will be put to forced labor.*

Let's Dig In

Nobody wants to be called slothful. It sounds gross, like slow-moving moss growing on a rock. Proverbs is blunt: the diligent get to lead, and the lazy get stuck. That's the deal. Ouch. That one stung.

Now, let's clear this up: diligence isn't the same thing as hustle culture. God's not asking you to grind yourself into exhaustion and brag about how busy you are. Diligence is steady faithfulness. It's showing up, even in the boring stuff. It's doing the things that need doing, without waiting for applause.

Laziness, on the other hand, doesn't always look like lying on the couch all day with Netflix asking, "Are you still watching?" Sometimes it's sneaky. It's procrastination. It's telling yourself you'll "get to it tomorrow" … and then tomorrow turns into next week… and suddenly it's three months later and the thing still isn't done. (Recall our chat about not relying on tomorrow?)

The truth is, diligence doesn't usually feel glamorous. Nobody's clapping for you because you folded the laundry, paid the bill on time, or knocked out that project at work. Those small, faithful choices add up. They build a life of stability and trustworthiness. They make you the kind of person people can count on. God sees every bit of it, even the stuff nobody else notices.

Here's the kicker: diligence honors God because it looks like Him. He's faithful. He finishes what He starts. He doesn't procrastinate His promises. When you live with diligence, you're reflecting His character in everyday life. That's a big deal!

So today, ask yourself: where has laziness been sneaking in? Where are you making excuses instead of progress? Don't wait for the "perfect moment" to start. Just take the next step. Wisdom says diligence pays off *always*. (Ask me tomorrow if I folded the laundry.)

Let's Reflect

- Where have you been putting things off that you know God wants you to handle?

- When has steady faithfulness paid off for you or someone you admire?

- What's one small, practical step of diligence you can take today?

Let's Pray

Lord, help me stop making excuses and start being faithful. Remind me that even small acts of diligence matter to You. Give me strength to show up consistently, even when it's not fun or glamorous, and let my everyday work reflect Your faithfulness. Amen.

Bottom Line

Excuses are busy talk while diligence is busy building.

Day 37 – *Generosity Wins*

Verse: Proverbs 11:25 - *Whoever brings blessing will be enriched, and one who waters will himself be watered.*

Let's Dig In

Generosity isn't just about handing someone a twenty or tossing coins into the open guitar case of a musician on a Times Square Subway platform. It's bigger than that. It's about living with open hands instead of clenched fists. Proverbs 11:25 tells us when you bless others, you get blessed too. When you water someone else, you don't run dry, you get watered right back. That's not karma. That's God.

The world says, "Hang onto what's yours. Don't give too much, you'll run out." God says the opposite: "Pour it out, and I'll handle the refill." That's scary sometimes, right? We like control. We like security. We like to know we'll have enough left over for ourselves. If God is who He says He is, then generosity is never a losing game.

I'll bet you've seen this in your own life. You show up for someone when you're tired, and somehow you leave more refreshed than when you came. You forgive someone who doesn't deserve it, and your own heart feels lighter. You give away your time, your encouragement, your resources, and instead of draining you, God finds a way to pour it back in.

Generosity also shuts down selfishness, which, let's be honest, we're all good at. Selfishness says, "What about me?" Generosity says, "God will take care of me, so I can take care of others." Here's the wild thing: every time you give, you're echoing God Himself. He's the ultimate Giver. He doesn't ration grace. He doesn't hold back. He pours it out freely, and He invites us to do the same.

Here's the bottom line: generosity wins. It blesses people around you, it refreshes your own soul, and it honors the God who gave everything for you. So, loosen the grip. Live open-handed. You won't regret it.

Let's Reflect

- When have you seen generosity refresh you instead of drain you?

- Where are you tempted to hold back when God's nudging you to give?

- What would living more open-handed look like in your daily life?

Let's Pray

Lord, thank You for being so generous with me. Help me quit living like I have to protect and hoard what You've given. Show me how to bless others with my time, my words, and my resources. Remind me that I'll never run out when I'm connected to You. Amen.

Bottom Line

Open hands, full heart. That's how generosity wins.

Day 38– *Justice Matters*

Verse: Proverbs 21:3 - *To do righteousness and justice is more acceptable to the Lord than sacrifice.*

Let's Dig In

It's easy to get caught up in looking "religious." Show up to church, sing the songs, check the boxes. None of that is bad, but Proverbs 21:3 cuts right through the motions: God cares more about how you actually live than the rituals you perform. Doing what's right and fair matters more to Him than any outward display. Sounds a bit obvious, no?

Think about it. You can drop money in the plate on Sunday and still treat people like garbage on Monday. You can volunteer at church but gossip about your neighbor. You can look squeaky clean on the outside but live with a heart that refuses to change. God's not impressed by appearances. He's after integrity.

Justice and righteousness aren't just big, churchy words, they show up on the daily. It's paying people what you owe them. It's telling the truth even when lying would be easier. It's refusing to look the other way when someone's being mistreated. It's standing up for what honors God, even if you're standing alone.

Here's the thing: sacrifice is easy if it doesn't cost us real change. Writing a check or showing up once in a while feels good, but it's surface-level if our hearts aren't in it. God says, "Don't give me your lip service, give me your life." #micdrop

So, ask yourself today: am I living in a way that honors Him, or am I just going through the motions? He doesn't want a performance. He wants your *whole self*: justice in your choices, righteousness in your relationships, integrity in the places nobody else sees.

Let's Reflect

- Where have you been tempted to look the part instead of living the part?

- What does justice look like in your everyday life?

- How does living with integrity show the world who God really is?

Let's Pray

Lord, keep me from going through the motions. Teach me to live with justice and righteousness in the everyday, not just in the easy moments. Help me care about what You care about and live in a way that reflects Your heart. Amen.

Bottom Line

God isn't after performance, He's after integrity.

Day 39 – *Wise Counsel*

Verse: Proverbs 15:22 – *Without counsel plans fail, but with many advisers they succeed.*

Let's Dig In

We all like to think we know best. We make plans, set goals, and convince ourselves we've got it handled. Proverbs 15:22 reminds us: going solo is like building Ikea® furniture with the instructions. Plans without wise counsel fall apart, but when you invite trusted voices in, success follows.

This isn't about asking every random person for input. Too many voices can be just as confusing as none at all. It's about seeking out people who love God, who live with integrity, and who care enough about you to tell you the truth, even when you don't want to hear it.

Let's be honest: sometimes we avoid wise counsel because we don't want to be told "no." We go shopping for opinions until we find someone who agrees with us. That's not counsel, that's confirmation bias. Real wisdom is being willing to hear what you don't want to hear, if it's coming from people grounded in God's truth.

Think about the last time you made a big decision. Did you pray about it? Did you ask anyone wise to weigh in? Or did you just go with your gut and hope it worked out? Wisdom says slow down. Invite others in. Humble yourself enough to realize you don't have all the answers.

Today's challenge: choose carefully, listen humbly, and weigh everything against God's Word. When all is said and done, the people you let speak into your life will shape your path. Wise counsel doesn't *replace* His voice; it helps tune your ears to it.

Let's Reflect

- Who do you turn to when you need wise counsel?

- When have you ignored advice and paid the price?

- How can you invite godly voices into a decision you're facing now?

Let's Pray

Lord, thank You for placing wise people in my life. Give me humility to seek their counsel and courage to listen, even when it's not what I want to hear. Help me filter every piece of advice through Your Word and trust that You guide me through both Your Spirit and Your people. Amen.

Bottom Line

Smart plans start with humble ears.

Day 40 – *Better a Little with God*

Verse: Proverbs 5:16 – *Better is a little with the fear of the Lord than great treasure and trouble with it.*

Let's Dig In

We live in a world that screams, "More is better." More money, more stuff, more recognition, more security. Proverbs cuts right through that noise: having a little with God is far better than having a lot without Him. (Lock in, this one's gonna be good.)

Think about how often we chase after the "more." A bigger house, a better car, a fatter bank account. None of those things are evil in themselves, but if chasing them costs you peace, integrity, or your walk with God, it's not worth it. Having the whole world means nothing if your soul is restless… or worse, lost.

The truth is, money and things can solve *some* problems, but they can't buy peace. They can't guarantee joy. They can't give you spiritual and emotional security that lasts past tomorrow. Plenty of people with great treasure still lie awake at night, anxious and unsatisfied. Proverbs tells us flat out: that kind of life comes with trouble.

On the flip side, you may not have much by the world's standards, but if you've got a heart anchored in the fear of the Lord, you're rich in the things that actually matter. Peace of mind. Contentment. The joy of knowing you're walking with Him. That's treasure no economy can touch. (There are those awesome words again: *a heart anchored in the fear of the Lord.*)

So, here's the challenge: stop measuring your life by what you can stack up. Start measuring it by Who you're walking with. Would you rather have a garage full of toys and a soul in chaos, or a simple life lived in step with God? Proverbs says the answer is obvious: *better a little with Him.* Always. Someone put that on a t-shirt.

Let's Reflect

- Where are you tempted to chase "more" instead of trusting God with "enough"?

- How have you experienced peace that money couldn't buy?

- What's one way you can practice contentment this week?

Let's Pray

Lord, thank You for reminding me that life isn't measured by what I own but by Whose I am. Teach me to be content with what You've given me, and keep me from chasing things that leave me restless and empty. Better a little with You than a lot without You. Amen.

Bottom Line

Peace with God is worth more than all the treasure in the world.

Day 41 – *Words for the Weary*

Verse: Proverbs 16:24 – *Gracious words are like a honeycomb, sweetness to the soul and health to the body.*

Let's Dig In

We've all had those days where one kind word felt like oxygen. You're running on empty, barely holding it together, and then someone drops a nugget of encouragement that lands like water in the desert. Proverbs 16:24 nails it: gracious words are sweet and healing. They're life-giving.

Now flip it. You've also had the other kind of day: when someone's words cut deep, or when criticism piled on top of everything else you were carrying. It's crazy how a single sentence can either lift you up or knock you flat. Words are powerful. Proverbs keeps circling back to that because God knows we underestimate it. Friends, we've discussed this a lot!

"Gracious" words don't mean fake compliments or sugary flattery. They mean words seasoned with kindness, patience, and truth. Sometimes that's encouragement. Sometimes it's correction, but always it's delivered with love. Either way, gracious words strengthen instead of crushing.

The tricky part? We don't always realize how heavy our words are. What feels like a throwaway comment to you might stick with someone else for years. I can still remember things people said to me decades ago, both the kind words that built me up and the harsh ones that left scars. Chances are, you can too.

This proverb is a reminder that we need to take our words seriously. We get to choose whether our mouth produces poison or honey. No, that doesn't mean we avoid hard truths. Sometimes the sweetest thing you can do for someone is to *lovingly* point them toward what's right. The delivery matters. Tone matters. Heart matters.

Think about Jesus. He could be blunt (ask the Pharisees) but with the broken and weary, He always spoke life. To the woman at the well, He told the truth, but with so much grace that she ran back to town transformed. That's honeycomb talk.

So, here's today's challenge: slow down and check your words. Are they fueling someone's soul or depleting it? Are they gracious, seasoned with patience, or sharp and careless? You may never know how much someone needed a gentle word that day, but God does. He can use *your* mouth to deliver it.

Let's Reflect

- Whose gracious words have refreshed you when you were weary?

- When have your own words healed (or harmed) someone?

- What's one way you can be intentional this week about speaking life to someone who needs it?

Let's Pray

Lord, thank You for the power of words. Forgive me for the times mine have torn down instead of built up. Teach me to speak with kindness and grace, even when I'm tired or frustrated. Use my words to bring healing and encouragement to people who need it most. Amen.

Bottom Line

Your words can be poison or honey; choose honey.

Day 42 – *Faithful Friends*

Verse: Proverbs 17:17 – *A friend loves at all times, and a brother is born for adversity.*

Let's Dig In

Proverbs 17:17 paints a simple but powerful picture: real friends show up. They don't just stick around when things are fun and convenient. They love at all times: through the highs, the lows, and all the messy in-betweens.

We throw the word "friend" around pretty lightly. Social media tells us we've got hundreds of them, yet when life falls apart, most of those "friends" are nowhere to be found. This proverb reminds us what *true* friendship looks like. It's steady. It's loyal. It doesn't disappear when things get hard.

Think about your closest relationships. Who are the people you can call at 2 a.m. when everything feels like it's crashing down? Who has stood with you in the middle of the storm, not trying to fix everything, just being there? That's a faithful friend. That's what Proverbs is pointing us toward.

There's another layer here too. "A brother is born for adversity." God designed family (and the family of faith) to be present in the hardest seasons. We're not built to go through life solo. Hard times are heavy, and trying to carry them alone will break you. That's why

God gives us friends and spiritual family who walk with us, shoulder to shoulder.

Friendship isn't just about who shows up for you, though. It's also about who *you're* showing up for. Are you the kind of friend who sticks around when things get uncomfortable, or do let the call go to voicemail? Do you love at all times, or only when it's easy? Faithful friendship is *mutual*: it's about giving as much as receiving.

Here's the encouragement: Jesus calls us His friends. He is the ultimate faithful friend, the One who never leaves, never bails, and never gets tired of showing up. Every human friendship will fall short at some point, but His never does. That truth frees us to be faithful to others without demanding perfection from them in return.

So, here's the challenge: take stock of your friendships. Thank God for the faithful ones who've stuck by you. Then ask yourself who needs you to be that kind of friend right now. Loyalty in friendships doesn't just bless the other person, it makes your life richer too.

Let's Reflect

- Who has been a faithful friend to you in the hard seasons?

- How have you seen God's faithfulness reflected through a friendship?

- What's one practical way you can show up for a friend this week?

Let's Pray

God, thank You for the gift of faithful friends. Help me not only to treasure them but to be one myself. Teach me to love at all times, not just when it's easy. Thank You for being the ultimate Friend who never leaves me. Amen.

Bottom Line

Real friends don't just show up for the party, they show up for the storm.

WEEK 7 – Living Legacy

The life you live today is the story they'll tell tomorrow.

Day 43 – *Guard Your Integrity*

Verse: Proverbs 10:9 – *Whoever walks in integrity walks securely, but he who makes his ways crooked will be found out.*

Let's Dig In

Integrity isn't flashy. Nobody's handing out trophies for telling the truth when lying would've been easier, or for keeping a promise when bailing would've saved you time. Yet Proverbs 10:9 tells us integrity is what gives you security. Walk straight, and you can hold your head high. Twist your path, and sooner or later, you'll get caught.

We live in a culture that prizes shortcuts. Cut corners, cover up mistakes, do whatever it takes to get ahead. The problem is, every shortcut leaves a crack. Eventually, those cracks show. Integrity doesn't mean perfection, it means consistency. Who you are when nobody's watching matches who you are when everybody's watching.

Walking in integrity gives you freedom. You don't have to remember which version of the story you told. You don't have to look over your shoulder, waiting for the lie to unravel. You can rest secure knowing *the truth will hold*, even if it costs you in the moment. That's peace money can't buy.

The opposite is exhausting. Living crooked, cutting corners, hiding secrets, pretending to be something you're not, it all eats away at you. Even if nobody else sees it yet, you know. Eventually, what's hidden in the dark always comes to light. Proverbs promises it: crooked paths get exposed.

So, today's wisdom challenge: how do we guard our integrity? By making small, daily choices that line up with God's truth. Tell the truth, even when it's uncomfortable. Follow through, even when it's inconvenient. Own your mistakes instead of covering them up. These little decisions stack up into a character that stands firm when life tests it.

Here's the bottom line: you can fake a lot of things, but integrity isn't one of them. Walk straight, and you'll walk secure.

Let's Reflect

- Where in your life do you feel most tempted to cut corners?

- How have you seen integrity bring peace and security?

- What's one small way you can guard your integrity this week?

Let's Pray

God, thank You for reminding me that integrity matters. Help me to walk straight even when shortcuts look easier. Give me the courage to tell the truth, follow through, and stay consistent so that my life reflects You. Amen.

Bottom Line

Shortcuts crack. Integrity holds.

Day 44 – *Fruitful Words*

Verse: Proverbs 15:4 - *A gentle tongue is a tree of life, but perverseness in it breaks the spirit.*

Let's Dig In

We've talked a lot about words in this study, and for good reason: they're often where our biggest struggles show up. Proverbs 15:4 gives us one more reminder: words can be a tree of life, or they can break the spirit. That's a heavy contrast.

A tree of life gives shade, fruit, and roots. It strengthens everyone who comes near. That's what gentle, godly words do. They refresh, they nourish, and they leave people better than they found them. Think about the times someone spoke encouragement into you right when you needed it. That one sentence may have carried you through a dark week.

On the flip side, words can break a spirit. Careless sarcasm, harsh criticism, gossip, or even silence when words of comfort were needed, they leave wounds. Sometimes the deepest scars aren't from actions but from sentences we replay in our heads for years. Proverbs is reminding us that our mouths can build or they can shatter.

Here's the part we can't ignore: once words are out, they don't come back. You can apologize, you can repent, and forgiveness can heal, but the words themselves can't be erased. That's why guarding your tongue matters so much. Words can give life or take it, and you get to choose which kind you'll plant.

So, maybe this is the best place to end, with today's challenge to *speak life*. You don't have to have all the answers, and you don't have to say much. Sometimes one gentle, thoughtful word is enough to change the course of someone's day, or even their life. That's the kind of fruit God is calling us to produce.

Let's Reflect

- Whose words have a tree of life in your own story?

- When have your words broken someone's spirit, and what did you learn from it?

- What's one way of being intentional this week about planting life-giving words?

Let's Pray

Lord, thank You for reminding me of the power of my words. Help me to plant life, not destruction. Teach me to speak with gentleness that refreshes and strengthens instead of wounding. Make my words a tree of life that reflects Your heart. Amen.

Bottom Line

If your words were fruit, would anyone want to eat them?

Day 45 – *Humility Before Honor*

Verse: Proverbs 18:12 - *Before destruction a man's heart is haughty, but humility comes before honor.*

Let's Dig In

Here's the truth: pride always struts in like it owns the room, and then it trips over its own shoelaces. Proverbs doesn't sugarcoat it: pride is a set-up for destruction. Humility, though? That's the ticket to real honor.

We don't like that. Pride feels good. Pride tells us we're in control, that we've got this, that we deserve recognition. What about humility? Humility sounds like weakness, like letting people walk all over you. Except that's not what humility *actually* is. Humility is *strength under control*. It's knowing who you are and Who you belong to, so you don't have to prove yourself every five minutes.

The problem with pride is that it blinds you. You can't see your own blind spots, you resist correction, and you start believing your own hype. Then, boom: the fall. Every single time. Ask anyone who's ever thought they were untouchable and watched it all unravel.

On the flip side, humility clears the air. A humble person isn't worried about appearances. They're teachable, they admit when they're wrong, and they don't need to push their way to the front of the line. They know God will honor them in His time. Here's the irony: those are the people we truly respect. Nobody enjoys hanging around a know-it-all. Everyone remembers the person who was kind, steady, and real.

This verse is basically saying: check your pride at the door. If you want the kind of honor that lasts, stop trying to manufacture it. Live humbly before God and let Him do the lifting. His timing, His way, His kind of honor. Pride gets you attention for a hot second. Humility earns you respect that sticks.

So, here's today's challenge: if you've been chasing the spotlight, maybe it's time to step out of it. If you've been pushing your way forward, maybe let God take the lead. Honor doesn't come from self-promotion; it comes from walking humbly and letting Him shine through you.

Let's Reflect

- Where's pride been sneaking into your life?

- Who do you know that carries themselves with true humility, and what stands out about them?

- What's one way you can choose humility this week, even if it costs you recognition?

Let's Pray

Lord, I know pride trips me up more than I like to admit. Pull me back when I start making it about me. Teach me to walk humbly so that any honor I receive points straight to You. Amen.

Bottom Line

Pride stumbles. Humility sticks the landing.

Day 46 – *Generational Faith*

Verse: Proverbs 13:22 - *A good man leaves an inheritance to his children's children, but the sinner's wealth is laid up for the righteous.*

Let's Dig In

When you hear the word inheritance, your mind probably goes straight to money, houses, or stuff passed down after someone's gone. Proverbs takes it deeper. It's not just about leaving your kids cash or property, it's about leaving them something that actually lasts. The best inheritance isn't sitting in a bank. It's faith lived out in front of them.

Think about Timothy in the New Testament. Paul pointed out that Timothy's sincere faith came from his grandmother Lois and his mother Eunice before it ever took root in him (2 Timothy 1:5). That's generational faith. Lois and Eunice probably weren't wealthy, but what they passed down changed the world through Timothy's ministry. Seriously, you can't put a dollar value on that.

Money fades. Houses crumble. Cars rust. Even the "valuable" stuff (jewelry, antiques, investments) eventually gets spent, lost, or passed on to someone who may not appreciate it. Faith, on the other hand, keeps paying *forward*. Every prayer whispered over your kids, every moment you model honesty when lying would've been easier, every time you forgive instead of holding a grudge, you're planting seeds that outlive you.

Here's the thing: this verse doesn't only apply if you have kids or grandkids. Legacy isn't limited to your bloodline. Everyone leaves fingerprints. You've got nieces, nephews, neighbors, students, coworkers, friends; someone is watching your life, whether you realize it or not. You're handing down an example every single day. The question is, what kind of inheritance are you leaving behind?

A "good" inheritance is more than words. It's lived out in the ordinary stuff. Kids (and anyone else watching) see whether your faith holds when life gets hard. They notice if you're generous or stingy, patient or short-tempered, forgiving or bitter. They see how you treat strangers, how you talk about people behind their backs, how you live when no one else is keeping score. That's the real legacy.

So, here's today's wisdom challenge: don't just think about what you'll leave behind in your will. Think about what you're leaving in people's hearts. Generational faith is worth more than anything money can buy, because it points people back to the God who never fails.

Let's Reflect

- Who passed faith down to you, and how has it shaped your life?

- What kind of spiritual inheritance do you want to leave behind?

- What's one practical way you can model faith this week to someone who's watching you?

Let's Pray

Lord, thank You for the people who handed faith down to me. Help me live in a way that plants seeds of faith in the next generation, whether that's my family, my friends, or anyone who crosses my path. Let my legacy point to You long after I'm gone. Amen.

Bottom Line

Money buys stuff that won't last. Faith is the gift that keeps on giving.

Day 47 – *The Joy of Wisdom*

Verse: Proverbs 3:13 - *Blessed is the one who finds wisdom, and the one who gets understanding.*

———————————————

Let's Dig In

Let's be real: most of the stuff we chase in life doesn't leave us blessed. We think a bigger paycheck will make us secure, or the right relationship will finally make us happy, or one more Amazon package will fill the hole. Spoiler alert: it never does. Proverbs 3:13 says the person who's truly blessed isn't the one with all the stuff, it's the one who finds wisdom.

Wisdom doesn't just make you smarter. It makes you steadier. It saves you from messes you could've avoided and helps you walk through the storms you can't. Wisdom gives you peace in the middle of chaos and joy in the middle of ordinary days. That's blessing.

Think about the difference between knowledge and wisdom. Knowledge is knowing the speed limit. Wisdom is slowing down anyway because you know a ticket isn't worth it, or worse, an accident. Knowledge fills your head. Wisdom changes your choices. When your choices line up with God's truth, life gets lighter. Joy creeps in, even in hard places, because you're walking in step with Him instead of stumbling around on your own.

Here's the thing: wisdom doesn't just fall out of the sky while you're scrolling your phone. You've got to seek it. You've got to want it. That means showing up in God's Word, listening to wise voices instead of the loud ones, and *actually* asking Him for it. The good news? James 1:5 says if you ask, He'll give it generously. He's not stingy with wisdom. He's thrilled to hand it out if we're humble enough to admit we need it.

I love how Proverbs says "finds wisdom." It's like a treasure hunt. You go looking, you dig deep, and when you uncover it, you realize it was worth every bit of effort. Unlike money, fame, or approval, wisdom doesn't drain you. It fills you. It blesses you. It makes life rich in ways the world can't touch.

So, here's today's encouragement and a challenge forever: stop chasing things that can't bless you. Start chasing wisdom like it's treasure, because it is. Blessed is the one who finds it, and that blessing is yours for the taking.

Let's Reflect

- When have you experienced joy as a direct result of a wise choice?

- What's one area of your life right now where you're desperate for God's wisdom?

- How can you keep chasing wisdom daily once this study wraps up?

Let's Pray

Lord, thank You that wisdom isn't hidden away but offered to me freely. Give me the humility to admit I need it and the hunger to keep chasing it. Let the joy of wisdom spill into my choices, my relationships, and my future. Amen.

Bottom Line

Wisdom is treasure, and the joy is finding it.

Day 48 – *Looking Back, Leaning Forward*

Reflection & application of all of these Proverbs.

Verse: Proverbs 19:20 - *Listen to advice and accept instruction, that you may gain wisdom in the future.*

Let's Dig In

Here we are: the second-to-last day. Feels weird, right? You've been walking through Proverbs for weeks now, and suddenly the finish line is in sight. Proverbs 19:20 is the perfect verse for this moment: "Listen to advice and accept instruction, that you may gain wisdom in the future."

This verse is a reality check. Wisdom isn't a one-and-done lesson you can check off like a to-do list. It's not, "Well, I did that Proverbs study, so I'm good for life." Nope. First of all, we only did a FEW Proverbs. Wisdom is a posture you carry into every season. Listening and accepting are daily choices that shape the person you're becoming.

So, let's look back for a second. What hit you hardest during this study? Was it something about your words? Your pride? Your plans? Your circle of friends? God doesn't poke at us randomly. If He pressed on something in your heart, it's because He wants to work on it. That conviction wasn't meant to shame you, it was meant to grow you.

Now let's lean forward. Listening is easy; we hear advice all the time. Accepting it? That's the kicker. Accepting means letting God's truth rearrange your priorities and change how you live. It means saying, "Okay, Lord, I hear You, and I'm actually going to do something about it." That's the kind of choice that keeps paying off years down the road.

This is your checkpoint, not your end point. Look back with gratitude for what God's already shown you. Lean forward with determination to keep listening, keep accepting, keep growing. Future-you will thank present-you for not stopping here.

Let's Reflect

- Which lesson from Proverbs has hit home the most for you and why?

- Where is God nudging you to keep listening and growing?

- What's one small step you can take to lean forward instead of drifting back?

Let's Pray

Lord, thank You for everything You've taught me through this study. Don't let it stop here. Help me to keep listening, keep accepting, and keep leaning forward into Your wisdom. Amen.

Bottom Line

Wisdom isn't a finish line, it's a lifestyle.

Day 49 – *Walking in Wisdom*

Verse: Proverbs 1:7 - *The fear of the Lord is the beginning of knowledge; fools despise wisdom and instruction.*

Let's Dig In

Do you remember way back on Day 1? We started here. Proverbs didn't ease us in gently, it threw us right into the deep end: "The fear of the Lord is the beginning of knowledge." Here we are again, 49 days later, circling back. Not because we ran out of verses, but because this is the anchor. The starting point. The foundation.

Everything we've studied: the words, the pride checks, the lessons on trust, humility, diligence, legacy, it all flows from this truth: wisdom starts with God. You can read all the self-help books, listen to every podcast, and memorize a thousand "life hacks," but without Him, it's just noise. Real wisdom begins when we stop pretending we've got it all figured out and bow to the One who actually does.

That phrase, "fear of the Lord," can sound intimidating. It's not about cowering, waiting for God to zap you with lightning. It's about reverence. It's about living with the deep awareness that He's God and you're not. It's about trusting His ways even when they clash with your own ideas of "reasonable." It's about believing His boundaries are for your good, even when you don't fully get them.

Here's the wild part: you've just spent seven weeks putting this into practice. Every time you wrestled with a proverb, every time you saw yourself in the reflection prompts, every time you prayed those real prayers, you were walking in wisdom. This isn't about filling a notebook. It's about reshaping how you live.

So, what happens now? You keep going. Wisdom isn't a season, it's a way of life. You'll still stumble. You'll still wrestle with pride, impatience, words that slip out too fast. Join the club. The point isn't perfection. The point is direction. You're walking in wisdom when you keep coming back to God as the source.

As this study wraps up, take a moment to celebrate. Not because you've "arrived," but because you've started. You've stepped onto the path Proverbs lays out, and that path leads to life. Stay on it. Revisit it. Keep walking in wisdom, step by step, day by day.

Let's Reflect

- Looking back, which lesson (or lessons) from this study do you want to carry forward daily?

- How can you remind yourself to come back to Proverbs regularly for refreshers?

- Who could you walk through this study with next so they experience this, too (and maybe bring you to a new level of wisdom-seeking)?

Let's Pray

Lord, thank You for walking with me through these past seven weeks. Thank You for every lesson, every conviction, every bit of wisdom You've given me. Keep me humble enough to keep learning, brave enough to keep applying, and faithful enough to keep walking with You every single day. Amen.

Bottom Line

Wisdom starts with God and walking with Him is how it lasts.

Epilogue: Still Going, Still Growing

If you've made it this far, then you know: Proverbs is not a one-and-done kind of study. It's a lifelong journey. These pages have only scratched the surface, and I'm so grateful you've walked through them with me.

For me, this project has been more than just another book. It's part of my own faith journey, one that's still unfolding. As I've begun my studies to become a Lay Deacon, I feel God pulling me even deeper into His Word. Proverbs has laid a foundation, but it's also pointed me upward and onward: to keep learning, to keep serving, and to let wisdom sink roots deep into my life.

My prayer is that this study won't end here for you either. Keep going. Keep opening your Bible. Keep laughing at yourself when God lovingly calls you out, and keep leaning on His grace that covers every stumble along the way.

Wisdom isn't about being perfect. It's about being teachable. It's about showing up, day after day, ready to hear what God has to say. Friend, if you keep showing up, God will keep shaping you. He's not done yet.

So, let's go forward together: a little wiser, a little braver, and a whole lot more anchored in Him.

Prayer to Carry Forward

Jesus, thank You for sticking with me through this journey. Every verse, every "ouch, that's me" moment, every laugh, every tear; you've been in it. I don't want to close this book and go back to the same old me. I want to keep leaning in, keep learning, keep letting Your wisdom change me from the inside out. Use what I've learned here to make me bolder in my faith and softer in my heart. Keep me teachable, Lord, because You're not done with me yet. Amen.

Bottom line

Wisdom is a journey, not a destination. Dear friend, the best part is, we get to walk it with Jesus leading the way.

My Blessing to You

Well, look at you, finishing strong! If you've hung with me through all these days in Proverbs, you're not the same girl who started. God's Word has this sneaky way of calling us out and building us up at the same time, and I know He's been doing both for you.

So, here's my blessing for you, friend: may you roll your eyes a little less at yourself, laugh a little more at God's sense of humor, and lean hard into His wisdom every single day. You don't have to nail it all, you just have to keep showing up. He'll do the rest.

Remember: Proverbs will call you out, but Jesus will lift you up. That's a combo worth living on repeat.

Visit favordeipress.com for

- Purchase links
- Promos and sales
- New and upcoming works
- Free journaling downloads
- Contact information
- Booking speaking engagements
- Booking book signing events